spenditude

\ 'spɛnditjud \

spenditude

\ ˈspɛnditjud \

A life-changing *attitude to money*

Paul Gordon & Janine Robertson

First published in 2020 by John Wiley & Sons Australia, Ltd

42 McDougall St, Milton Qld 4064

Office also in Melbourne

Typeset in 11.5/14pt Palatino LT Std Light

© John Wiley & Sons Australia, Ltd 2020

The moral rights of the authors have been asserted

ISBN: 978-0-730-37203-5

 A catalogue record for this
book is available from the
National Library of Australia

Cover design by Wiley

Cover image: © VasutinSergey / Shutterstock; Visual Generation / Shutterstock

Internal icons: © Decorwithme/Shutterstock; tkacchuk/Getty Images; VasutinSergey / Shutterstock; Visual Generation / Shutterstock

10 9 8 7 6 5 4 3 2 1

Disclaimer

The material in this publication is of the nature of general comment only, and does not represent professional advice. It is not intended to provide specific guidance for particular circumstances and it should not be relied on as the basis for any decision to take action or not take action on any matter which it covers. Readers should obtain professional advice where appropriate, before making any such decision. To the maximum extent permitted by law, the authors and publisher disclaim all responsibility and liability to any person, arising directly or indirectly from any person taking or not taking action based on the information in this publication.

Contents

Acknowledgements   *ix*
Foreword   *xi*
Introduction   *xiii*

1   What's my spenditude?   1

2   Dozy, sleepy, drowsy and weary   29

3   Where did the time go?   49

4   The voice inside my head   59

5   The *why* factor   87

6   Where's the tiger?   107

7   This intelligence isn't artificial   137

8   What could possibly go wrong?   157

9   Under the spreadsheets   171

10   A bit on the side (and the future of work)   189

11   Rewirement   205

The beginning   217
About the authors   221
Index   223

**good
return**

**From every copy sold, the authors will donate 50 cents
to Good Return.**

Breaking the poverty cycle starts with awareness of your
attitude to money.

Good Return helps people build pathways out of poverty
through access to responsible finance, financial education
and business skills.

For more information, visit goodreturn.org.au

\ 'spenditjud \

adjective. Your attitude to money.

Those with good spenditude end up with more financial security and peace of mind.

Acknowledgements

I'd like to thank my three beautiful sons, Ben, Liam and Marcus, for their inspiration and creative support. They make me proud every day.

A final thank you to my dear dad who has been a great inspiration all my life.

—Paul

There is no greater anchor in my life than my husband, Bow, whom I adore. We have a busy life with three young kids and you put my desire to write this book first. Thank you.

I hope that this book can inspire our children, Hugh, Ned and Elise—to have great spenditude and to pursue their own purpose. All my love.

—Janine

Foreword

Are some people just smarter than others when it comes to money? Or is it more that they found some secret formula early and have stuck with it? Is it habits, willpower or ego? What's the secret formula, please? I want what they're having!

Basically, spenditude has nothing to do with your age, your stage in life or your income. The secret is more about re-training your brain to think differently about money. Simple to say, but trickier to do. Until now!

This book explores the formula for financial wellbeing—money and purpose—and describes how we can rewire our brain to significantly enhance our overall sense that 'we will be okay'.

'I have peace of mind because I consider the future'; 'I can make choices'; 'I am free to create the life I want'.

Everyone has their own version of financial freedom and choice. Doors close on us. Life changes and the stress of living in this fast-paced, crazy twenty-first century all get in the way. Only about one in five of us experience financial freedom—so what are the rest of us doing wrong?

We'll describe how people who are 'good with money' have formed their habits and rituals, which is what delivers their financial outcomes. This is not about get-rich-quick tactics, but about exploring attitudes to money. We want to provide you with evidence that your financial future is absolutely in your hands. It's not about doing things differently; it's about thinking things differently. We want you to tell your brain not to listen to your old money story.

We also acknowledge that everyone has a different purpose and that money means very different things to all of us. So we won't be encouraging you to become wealthy or savvy. We'll encourage you to connect your brain with your purpose. Money is simply an enabler, not the main game.

A big thanks to all the people we interviewed who have shared their expertise, their personal stories and their aspirations and dreams. You helped us to confirm our hypothesis: that our spenditude is not based on our parents, our age or stage of life. We are all very different and our life stories are unique. Each case study in the book is a true story of life events, money, motivation and purpose. Our experts have generously shared their knowledge and wisdom. Thank you again.

Our wish for this book is twofold. First, for you to find the formula that will flick that switch inside your brain. Second, that the book gets shared around with those you love so they can flick their own switch.

Janine and Paul

Health warning: *Do not* change any of your money habits until you have read the whole book. Keep spending. If you try to change your spenditude along the way, it won't work.

Introduction

Have you ever tried to delete an app on your phone and observed how all the apps start to shake?

Imagine those shaking apps as representing the different parts of your life ... out of control and wobbling away.

Now think of the main three apps on your home screen as the most important aspects of your life. They represent health, money and relationships. If all three are wobbling, you're in trouble. You can hit the 'reset' button—but deep inside you know they're still wobbling.

The aim of this book is to stabilise your money app, which will hopefully have a positive impact on your health and relationships. Stabilising your money app means changing old habits, and to successfully change your behaviour you need to have a goal, a reward or some form of incentive—and we're not talking about greed. Greed lacks purpose. We believe the best incentive is the desire to create a life that provides you with greater peace of mind, the ability to make good decisions, the freedom of choice, and a sense that your effort is rewarded and that your loved ones will be okay financially. Our premise is that it's your *attitude* to money that has the greatest impact on your financial outcome. Change what's within and the external world reflects it. A New Reality.

So what can you do to stop your money app from shaking?

Do you think some people are 'better with money'? That they appear to have a good feel for it and make better financial decisions?

Is it genetics, parental upbringing, good habits or just good luck?

We believe it's none of these things and all of these things.

Your behaviour towards money is formed when you're young (under 10) and develops as you experience life.

By 20 most of us have a default setting for our attitude to money. This isn't particularly apparent to us; however, it drives your spending and saving decisions from an early age.

Parents have some impact as they're our largest influence in the early years, but it's not just them. Genetics plays a part, although it's not the main influence. Having good habits is a by-product of your attitude to money. And good luck seems to happen when people put themselves in a position to receive it.

The three questions to ask are:

1. What is my attitude to money?
2. Can I re-shape it to serve me better (because I feel I can do a lot better)?
3. Is it too late?

These are the questions we'll focus on. We'll delve into your brain to work out why you're the way you are and how you could change.

We'll then start to explore behaviour-changing habits and techniques that will enhance your financial wellbeing.

Is it too late? Never. Most of us will live well into old age, so the sooner you start changing your habits the better.

We'll learn from real people—experts in their field who have kindly shared their knowledge.

So strap yourself in for a habit-changing experience with two differences. The first difference is we don't want you to change anything until you've finished reading the book; and the second difference is we won't focus on greed.

We'll concentrate on resetting your money app (your spenditude) so you can enjoy more freedom, choice and contentment.

We'll focus on habit change so you can live a more fulfilled life. If greed is your bag, then you'll also benefit from being better with money.

We've unearthed a set of New Realities that will lay out a path for you to make the habit changes that will empower you to live the life you want.

Why bother changing? To answer that question, you need to ask yourself one simple question: 'In your life right now, what could possibly go wrong?'

Think hard. It's not a trick question.

Once you've answered that question we know you'll be keen to read on. But first we'd like to acquaint you with the steps you'll be taking through this book.

The steps to your New Reality

Habit change is a tricky business. Think of all the times you've attempted a significant habit change. What were the formulas for success (or failure)? Our strategy for habit change is threefold:

1. Set a goal and a reward.
2. Have a simple track to follow.
3. Don't do anything until you finish reading this book.

By the conclusion of the book you'll have picked up 11 New Realities (one for each chapter). We'll ask you to identify your motivation to change and act. This is why we ask you to wait until the end—because these 11 realities are interdependent. It's our simple path for you to follow. Each reality takes you towards the beginning of a new relationship with money.

We hope you enjoy collecting these New Realities and that you get to a great place where choice is more abundant, decisions are easier, there's less stress and you discover a new peace of mind around your finances. Just imagine if your relationship with money was aligned with your purpose.

Worth attempting, we think.

Chapter 1

What's my spenditude?

Spenditude. Strange word, isn't it?

It's the collision of two words to form a description that packs two meanings into one: **spend**er and att**itude**. A bit like glamping, frenemy, staycation, chillax … If we merge these words, we find the difference between those who create wealth and the rest of us, who just get by, thinking we're doing okay … but not really doing okay.

Why should I care about my spenditude?

Your spenditude determines your overall financial position. It's the difference between making informed money decisions and poor ones. It dictates the types of choices you can make in your life and assists you in having peace of mind and a higher level of contentment. So spenditude (your attitude to money) is quite a force of nature.

Imagine if you could break a long-term cycle of spending and start creating financial security. A chance to take money off the table as a worry item in your daily life. And imagine if you could harmonise your attitude with that of your spouse/partner.

Now imagine if you could identify your kids' attitude to money and set them on a path they will thank you for later. Exploring your spenditude will lead you along a journey of discovery.

We're living in a consumer society that can be draining both financially and emotionally. Many of us get stuck, not wanting to take a step out of our comfort zone and thinking, 'I coulda' or 'I shoulda'. Our behaviours can be repetitive and automatic.

Staying on the money treadmill means nothing changes, so we'll look to the *why* factor: *why* do you have this attitude? Is it genetic, taught or acquired? Can you change it or is it in your familial or cultural DNA? How can you find the insights and wisdom, the deep motivators that drive your spenditude? How can you give yourself the best chance of success?

Just one thing...

You shouldn't stop your spending behaviours until you've finished reading this book.

In his book *Allen Carr's Easy Way to Stop Smoking* the author asks the reader to continue smoking while reading the book. He goes on to say that after you finish reading the book you won't feel like smoking! And we want to send that same message: maintain your spenditude until the end of the book.

P.S. If you want to quit smoking, check out Allen's book. It's seriously effective.

At this stage we don't want you to think that you'll become one of *those* people. You know the ones: tight-arse, always worrying where every cent is going, frugal and boring. No. We want you to have fun and be in a position to have financial freedom. The freedom to live the life you want with less stress.

Identifying your spenditude

Let's have a look at a pair of identical twins whose different spenditudes resulted in their lives being not so identical.

The sibling test

Jeff and Graham. Men approaching retirement age. Baby boomers. Identical twins with identical childhoods and similar experiences. They both worked in government jobs as soon as they graduated from high school. They were smart and had a great childhood in a working-class suburb with parents who provided them with everything they needed to access education and live a safe life.

Fast forward 40 years to when the twins are about 60.

Jeff lives in an affluent suburb, owns his house and has two investment properties. He considers real estate to be a bit of a hobby and keeps an eye on the market. He's worked hard, saved hard and plans to retire from his steady job (which he's had virtually all his life) on his sixtieth birthday. He thinks he'll work as a consultant for six months of the year and spend time travelling the other half of the year.

(continued)

The sibling test *(cont'd)*

Graham is renting a nice little apartment in a suburb further away from the city. He doesn't have any plans to retire yet and is still working 50 hours a week. He's had a great career, shifting jobs, getting promotions and 'climbing the ladder'. Yet, he hasn't built up any real assets and is looking at the prospect of working until he drops. He's about to lease a luxury car so he can appear as successful as his brother.

Here's the rub. Graham has earned significantly more than Jeff over the years.

Two identical human beings who wound up not identical.

Jeff's attitude to money served him very well while Graham's didn't. What happened?

Identifying your spenditude is the first step to understanding what happened to the twins.

There's significant evidence that your spenditude will dictate your financial outcome. It's not what we earn or how old we are—it's how we feel about money that matters. It's your attitude to money. If your attitude is to spend to make you feel good or look good, then you're probably sharing Graham's journey.

If your attitude is more about surviving and 'just getting there' you probably feel frustrated about money. And you're not alone—that's the majority of the population!

If you're sorted, feel in control, have a sense of financial security and are instinctively good with money, then you're probably sharing Jeff's journey.

So what happened? How did Graham end up with an attitude to money that was directly the opposite of his twin's?

We all have habits, rituals and attitudes towards money. Some of us are naturally good with money, while others have no real interest in money and use it as a means to an end. Most of us sit in the middle, where we would prefer to be in a better position but aren't sure how to 'flick the switch'.

The three categories of spenditude

Let's introduce the three categories of spenditude — Spender, Slender and Defender — and start to consider where we fit.

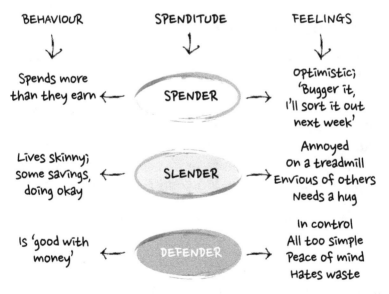

BEHAVIOUR	SPENDITUDE	FEELINGS
Spends more than they earn ←	SPENDER →	Optimistic; 'Bugger it, I'll sort it out next week'
Lives skinny; some savings, doing okay ←	SLENDER →	Annoyed On a treadmill Envious of others Needs a hug
Is 'good with money' ←	DEFENDER →	In control All too simple Peace of mind Hates waste

What spenditude do you have? Perhaps you see yourself as a hybrid or on the cusp? This will become clearer as we delve into the deep values and motivators that form your spenditude.

Defenders are people who are simply good with money. One of the twins, Jeff, is clearly a Defender. Defenders have a filter over their eyes as they spend. This filter is a combination of 'Do I need it now? Is it the right price? Can I get a discount? Is it tax effective? Which account will I use? Will it put me under my safety threshold?' and so on.

Spenders are the ones with the flash cars, the newest iPhone, no virtual filter over their eyes and certainly no focus. They treat money as a means to an end. Graham is a Spender.

The majority of us are Slenders—we're conscious of money but could be doing so much more to improve our situation and become secure in our financial futures.

A bit about behaviour

Behaviour—not what you earn—has the biggest impact on your financial outcomes.

A 2018 study by an Australian bank confirmed that your financial wellbeing isn't about what you earn, but how you think about money. In fact, your salary only accounts for 7 per cent of the influence on overall outcomes, whereas your behaviour and attitude account for up to 61 per cent!

This attitude to money is what influences your financial outcomes and it's often overlooked in financial literacy education and self-help books. The 61 per cent is the key that flicks the switch. Improving your attitude to money and money habits is the basis of this book.

Before we describe in detail the three categories of spenditude that people can fall into, here's a conversation that one of this book's authors overheard. See if you can identify with any of these people.

A spenditude conversation

A Spender, a Slender and a Defender walked into a bar…
well, they were actually in a restaurant, but anyway … and
a spenditude conversation broke out.

It was around 10.30 pm and the table behind me at a busy restaurant was full of what I heard to be young 30-somethings. They were talking about money. Not in a crass or boasting way, but in a more deep and personal way. My ears pricked up and I started to eavesdrop.

The group was talking about a friend (Michael) and saying he earns over $5000 a month — however, he admits he spends way more than that (he doesn't know exactly how much). The group was shocked and considered him to be 'crazy'. They didn't seem to understand how this was even possible.

One member of the group (Tim) said, 'I am not happy at work. I took the job because financial stability is very important to me. Although I am not happy, I will not leave.' The group responded with a feeling of understanding, though some were not impressed by the decision to stick around doing something he was not enjoying because 'life is too short'.

Another guy (Andrew) said, 'Before I got married I wanted to share my money beliefs with my partner (Lucy). I talked to her about how I see money and then I showed her an Excel spreadsheet that described how I keep in the black. She was instantly curious (which surprised me) and started to muck around with the spreadsheet and much to her surprise she was able to figure out how to move from the red to the black. She was hooked from that day on and I was so relieved.'

(continued)

A spenditude conversation *(cont'd)*

The conversation continued and it was surprising to hear these 30-somethings being so open about their financial positions, stories and ways of doing things. This is generally a topic that we think of as taboo and often we would not risk the judgement of our peers by being so open.

What they discussed in that 15 minutes was the essence of this book. Everyone has a different relationship with money and this affects their lives and beliefs. Andrew was clearly a Defender and keen to teach his partner Lucy (a Slender) some valuable lessons so they could live a harmonious and financially secure life together. If Lucy had rejected Andrew's spreadsheet there may have been some trouble ahead!

Michael was judged because he spent more than he earned. Michael, like our twin Graham, is a Spender.

Andrew displayed deep money values around financial stability that had a significant impact on his life choices. He is a Defender although he is also trapped in his own money beliefs.

So in a short period of time I was able to hear the stories of a Spender, a Slender and a Defender. Let's look at their spenditude more closely. See if you can identify with one of them. Think of your loved ones as well.

Spenders

Spenders are always having a great time but have no thoughts about where the money is coming from or how it will affect them later.

Spenders make up around 20 per cent of the population.

They love to use money to gain experiences. An experience could be dinner, an Uber trip or travel.

Big items and small are all dealt with in similar fashion. There's no sense of awareness of money and they tend to hate being brought to account by loved ones. Spenders could be high income earners, not earn an income or be anywhere in between. Financial advisers have many anecdotes about clients who earn a very high salary and manage to spend well over this (like Michael from the restaurant). These clients are often unaware of how much they spend.

On the other side of the income divide, Spenders can be on social benefits, and spend it all the day they receive it. In marriages, Spenders can cause all sorts of trouble if they are married to a non-Spender.

The feelings of a Spender tend to be optimistic, careless, easygoing, reckless and instantly gratified, loving fun, denial and being unaware of their financial position. Or they could just be someone who has a deep-seated value that 'I earn it so I can spend it how I like'.

Spenders have fun until the music stops. When the money and the access to credit is cut off they tend to be quite exposed. Spenders who are retrenched tend to panic and go after the next job available. Spenders also tend to move jobs regularly, chasing down more income.

Spenders can change their spenditude and create sustainable financial outcomes. Their biggest hurdle is themselves. They don't generally want to change anything. The key is to make it feel like they're not forgoing lifestyle. It's like having your cake and eating it too.

Retail therapy

Some say over-spending is an addiction. If so, addiction theory is changing. It's not the chemical hook that makes a heroin addict, it's the status of their life. Tests prove that the happier you are with your life, the less likely you are to be an addict. So if you feel you need retail therapy to feel good (or you're living with someone like that) then this insight is of particular relevance. Make your inner self happier and you may just put down the credit card.

Let's take a peek inside the Spender's brain:

Slenders

Slenders have a clear list of values, all equally weighted with no specific focus.

This is the majority of the population. Slenders have some Spender and some Defender habits, but here's the thing:

they're frustrated that they could be doing better and envious that others are getting ahead of them. And social media and FOMO (fear of missing out) don't help!

Slenders want more but tend to get stuck in the day-to-day humdrum. A Slender's brain is orderly, but there's not much focus. Here's what it looks like:

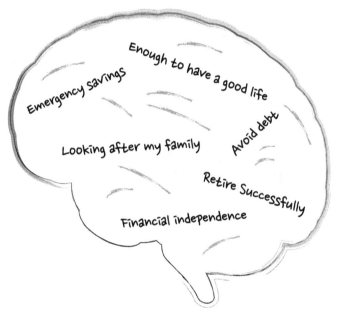

Defenders

Defenders have clear focus, know where their money is and are mindful about how they use it.

They have 20/20 vision and they can't understand how someone could possibly spend more than they earn. They can sometimes be procrastinators when it comes to spending — trying to make sure they're using their value lens, which can be frustrating for people around them. (A value lens means every purchase is viewed with a formula of 'Do I need it now?', 'How am I going to fund this?', 'Can it wait?', 'Is it the right price?', 'What about a discount?', 'Is it tax effective?', 'Which account will I use?', 'Will it put me under my safety threshold?') But the flip side of not making quick money decisions may be a sense of being more mindful about purchases and ensuring they're true to their values, plans and goals.

Defenders make up around 15 to 20 per cent of the population. Let's take a look inside their brain:

Focus

When you study these three brains, the one big message is focus. Spenders have no focus and Defenders are very focused — but more than that, they are focused on their deep values. This defines their relationship with money.

So the big questions are:

Can a Spender or a Slender become a Defender?

Can a Defender get lost in their focus and forget to enjoy their financial independence?

Is it too late to change?

Does a Spender lose the fun out of buying stuff if they change?

Will a Slender be able to commit to change and develop the focus required?

If you think about life, most of us are given the chance to earn money. Some get it through privilege of family, culture or economic environment; others have to work harder to achieve the baseline. If you have the honour of being able to earn money, then you have two choices: earn it and create your own version of financial security and independence, or don't. It's that simple! Defenders choose the former, while Spenders go the other way. The Slender in the middle is like a middle child (both authors are middle children and can relate). The Slender struggles to enjoy the thrill of spending and doesn't receive the gains of financial independence.

If you identified as a Defender, well done. Your next challenge is to fine-tune your skills and continue to review your situation. You're in a position to make choices, consider more sophisticated financial strategies and really create the life you want. However, many Defenders get a bit too caught up with their money values and forget to enjoy the journey. This is where Defenders could fine-tune their money narrative.

If you identified as a Slender, don't despair — you're not far off being a Defender and we'll provide you habit-changing tactics as you attempt to flick the switch in your brain.

For Spenders, the message is more fundamental:

- Do you enjoy being a Spender?
- Do you worry that one day it might all come crashing down?
- Have you stopped reading because this stuff scares you?

Spenders can change, but they need different tactics from Slenders. For Spenders, it's a journey where we combine lifestyle and baby steps to change rather than a more aggressive move towards Defender. Many of you reading this book may know a Spender, so perhaps read on for their sake (as they may not read this themselves).

There are many Defenders who love to spend and live life to the full. Not all of them are tight-arses. They get all the excitement of a Spender while still holding true to their core money values.

So Spenders, don't let the door slam in your face — flick that switch so you can live the life you want knowing you'll have new power to make better choices and more freedom to enjoy your life.

Any behaviour change ultimately starts with a *why*. The trigger (your personal why) may be a door slamming (divorce, retrenchment or illness, for example) or it may be an awareness of your position and a desire for change.

Paul's story

My spenditude has changed since my divorce, so I will share both. Divorce, or any major life event, can rock your values, and change your needs and drivers — and your spenditude. It was a big door-slamming moment for me and my family.

Pre-divorce

I have three boys and an ex-wife who was definitely a Defender when I met her. My money narrative back then (prior to 2010) was:

Values: Appearing financially successful, looking after my kids. I earn it so I can spend it how I like.

Needs: Living comfortably and having an enjoyable life.

Drivers: Making as much money as I can.

Spenditude: No surprises. I was a classic Spender. This spenditude did me no favours post-divorce. My ex-wife was the Defender anchor that kept us moored safely away from my Spender habits. We had some great holidays and the kids did not do without. However, post-divorce my spenditude ship almost sank.

As with major life events, they tend to come in threes. Not only did my marriage end but I also lost my beautiful brother to cancer and then lost my job — all in an 18-month period. What I realised is my underlying money value was to be there for my kids. This is what stressed me most as I was sinking and that was going to affect them.

(continued)

Paul's story *(cont'd)*

I am now a Slender on the cusp of Defender (with some Spender still inside my being that's not allowed out as much).

The present

In my case, a significant life event (a big door closing on me) shook me up — it changed my values, my needs and my drivers. I needed to change my habits. It is still a journey. I was a Spender and loved it. I now see that I had to change if I was going to be true to myself.

Don't wait for the door to close on you as it's not likely to be much fun, and remember that it may come in threes.

I now focus on experiences, not possessions. Much better!

Spenditude feelings and habits

Feelings often drive our behaviours. It's important to reflect on feelings, as this is your first line of decision making—we feel decisions before we choose them. Don't let feelings prejudice your ability to improve your spenditude.

Here are some examples of how your feelings and spenditude drive your habits.

Spenders

This is a minority group. Their spenditude doesn't always serve them.

Shopaholics, retail-therapy lovers, those addicted to the thrill of the spend and impulsive people are all good descriptions of a Spender.

We all have a bit of Spender in us, but what defines a true Spender is their lack of remorse at spending. They like to spend and they use debt or other people's money if they don't have the cash available.

Spenders can be high-income earners. They earn a lot and they spend more. It's a state of mind but also a habit that can be broken. But it's a difficult one for Spenders to break because they're having so much fun … until the music stops. Slam!

Spender feelings

- I earn it and can spend it however I like.
- Life's too short to worry about money (however, Spenders worry in their quiet moments).
- It won't happen to me.
- Don't talk to me about my money habits—don't judge me.
- I want to look successful.
- I'm blindly optimistic.
- My parents were tight and that's not me.
- Money is boring.
- I don't understand or care much about money.
- I hate tax time.
- I'm envious of those who are good with money but I haven't changed my habits.

Spender habits

- They spend more than they earn: 'I'll deal with the consequences later.'
- They're unaware of cashflow.
- They have no self-control over their spending: 'I need it now.'

- They don't accumulate.
- They rely on borrowing to create their lifestyle.
- They're unlikely to consider changing their spenditude.
- They're vulnerable to life events.
- They have FOMO and want to keep up with others.
- They look for easy money (Bitcoin, lotto wins, etc.).
- They're unlikely to have a will.

Slenders

This is the middle group. Just like a middle child, they're frustrated and feel left out:'I do all the right things but don't seem to get ahead.'

The best description is feeling like you're on a treadmill or conveyor belt.

Slenders feel frustrated and annoyed. They're time poor, busy, stressed, living from month to month, coping, compliant, paying off debt on time, limited savers and tired.

As they make up the majority of the population (approximately 60 per cent), Slenders are the target for self-help books and financial budgeting workshops, and could be vulnerable to unscrupulous money schemes.

To this end, they really do want to improve and they have the best chance of improving their spenditude if they change their habits.

Slender feelings

- I do the right thing but I'm not getting ahead.
- I'd like financial security.
- I need a hug.
- I feel guilty.

- I find talking about money stressful.
- More money would solve my problems.
- I'm doing okay, but I want to do more.

Slender habits

- They worry about retirement savings and money in general.
- They can be envious, frustrated, anxious and concerned.
- They're always looking for a magic formula.
- They continually want to do better with money.
- They don't like debt.
- They have a sense of what they earn and how they spend it.
- They reluctantly borrow (but are keen to pay back).
- They attempt to do the right thing financially.
- They live skinny.
- They occasionally focus on being a Defender but tend to fall back to Slender.
- They have some savings but are concerned that it's not enough.
- They're conservative about money.
- They're prepared to spend money to have the good life.
- They may have investments but don't have much of a plan.
- They want to be a role model for their kids.
- They're keen to give to charity but hesitant to over-extend on donations.
- They're influenced by others.
- They may have a will and insurance to protect their income and assets.

Defenders

These people are simply 'good with money'. They make up 15 to 20 per cent of the population (maybe less).

This spenditude is the envy of Slenders. Spenders, however, just don't get them. Defenders like to spend but always look for value. They may have fun, but they delay gratification. They know where their money is and are aware of their cashflow and debt. They understand tax and minimise it; they use reward programs, hate waste and look for bargains.

What a Defender possesses that the other two behaviour types don't is a value lens. Imagine this lens over your eyes; it works in milliseconds and is set up all the time. This lens calculates value on any financial decision (we all want this lens).

Defenders can be born that way or they can acquire the skill. It can be fine-tuned if parents are Defenders—but not always. It's a behaviour hard wired into their DNA. And they don't understand Spenders or Slenders.

Defender feelings

- I want financial security.
- I hate waste.
- I know I'm good with money.
- I'm constantly learning about money.
- I find money interesting and an enabler.
- I have peace of mind that I'm okay for the future.
- I'm proud of my achievements.
- I could do better (Defenders are competitive with themselves).

Defender habits

- They're aware of their cashflow at all times.
- They like to spend where they see value.
- They have a plan.
- They understand the system (tax, rewards, timing, compound interest, etc.).
- They borrow to create wealth.
- They never borrow to deflate wealth.
- They practise delayed gratification.
- They may be tight-arses (but not always).
- They seek advice to fine-tune their ideas or test them with an expert.
- They're legacy builders.
- They think before making financial decisions.
- They talk about money with their kids.
- They have a detailed estate plan including insurance to protect income and assets.
- They can be stuck because they won't spend money.

A Spender named Anna (part 1)

Anna's parents never spoke about money—there was no need as they had plenty of it.

With two high-functioning parents, she didn't see much of her mum and dad, who both worked long hours. Anna had lots of extended family around—aunties and uncles, cousins and grandparents—who provided for her and her brother on a day-to-day care basis. As a child, it was easy for Anna to see that you could have money without love or love without money.

When Anna's parents moved her family to another city due to work, she missed her large extended family. Her parents compensated for their lack of availability by providing a stream of unlimited funds and she became a (self-described) spoiled brat.

At 14 Anna moved back to live with her aunt and uncle. She still had access to money, but her relatives expected a lot more from her (like helping around the house) than her parents had. It was a tough change, but she was happy to be 'back home'. Not long after the move, her grandfather passed away. Upon cleaning out his home they discovered a tax debt of $70 000. This was the first time Anna realised the difficulty that not having money could cause; his house had to be sold against the wishes of his 13 children.

Anna finished school and spent a gap year in South America. Her spending ways continued. She was the life of the party: she always had cash to buy the next round, a great gift or petrol for a road trip. Despite her parents building a brand-new home for her, she wanted to travel and make some decisions about what to do next.

While her parents wanted her to have a career, their ultimate goal was her happiness and they provided funds to help her make choices—paying for her travel, rent and other needs up until her mid twenties, and providing her with a credit card to manage her spending.

While she was in Paraguay, Anna's host family provided another money lesson. Income wasn't consistent for the family and one night there were no funds for a meal. They asked Anna to help. It was a wake-up call. To ask for money was very hard. Papa was a proud man who took care of his family. Once again, the message was clear: if your family had time available, then money was likely to be an issue.

Anna was a self-described Spender. Throughout her childhood and right up until her mid twenties she had no reason to consider value, or even cost. Her spending was all about lifestyle. Driving her spenditude was instant gratification, with no requirement to take responsibility. Despite a couple of lessons affecting her values, she had no reason to move away from her Spender habits.

But then, when she was in her mid twenties, a big door slammed shut … and her habits had to shift.

More about Anna and her change later …

A Slender named Jenny

Jenny's parents worked hard for their money, as did their parents before them, and their parents before them. Money was something that never really came easy.

When interest rates hit 18 per cent in the 1980s the pressure to pay the mortgage and bills was enormous. Jenny remembers her parents emptying her money box and tracking every cent. The bills were documented with care. Lights were never left on. If you were cold, you put on a jumper. Clothes were handed down from siblings and cousins. There were no meals out and social events were held at home or picnics in the park.

While Jenny never felt she went without, she knew money was tight—and she has a school workbook that proves it: 'If I had some money I would pay off the mortgage for Mum' was the story she wrote at age seven.

Money became less stressful for a while when Jenny's mum went back to work. She worked weekends to get some extra money while Jenny's dad looked after the kids. Her mum missed most of the netball games, visits to see nanna and social events.

The clear message was that you had to make sacrifices and work hard in order to get ahead. Her parents saved and continued to work hard and were able to make some improvements on their home.

When Jenny was 15 she got her first part-time job. Her money was almost entirely disposable: fun with friends, clothes, a bit of savings so she could take a holiday at the end of school.

Jenny finished school, went to uni, got married, bought a house and had kids. The typical and expected behaviour. While her parents had shown her that hard work and awareness of your finances kept your family secure, money wasn't really discussed and she had no real understanding of how to manage her finances.

Jenny thinks she's okay with money, but her husband just doesn't get it. He loves the finer things in life. His attitude is that 'things have a way of working out'—and it drives her crazy. He has little awareness of their financial position and happily spends money on the kids, eating out, holidays and upgrading technology. His idea of a budget is that the ATM dispensed cash or the credit card wasn't declined. Meanwhile, Jenny is stressed about the mortgage and bills and hardly ever buys a coffee. She feels like she's living a similar life to her parents, which isn't so bad. She can never work out why her best friend seems to have more (despite her friend's lower income) and thinks that it would be really nice to have a bit more disposable cash.

Jenny has no clear focus or plan. She wants to make sure she's responsible with her money but also wants to enjoy her life. Her kids and family are the most important thing. Jenny is happy but can see that she's repeating the patterns of generations of her family.

A Defender named Tom

Tom grew up in a family where money was in short supply. His mum worked in a factory environment and his dad was not around. Their home was in a tower block of government housing alongside other low-income families. English was his mum's second language.

Tom never received regular pocket money, but he was encouraged to save coins in his money box. His mum was a bargain hunter, always looking for items that were discounted, buying in bulk and saving throughout the year to make sure there was money for Christmas and birthdays. Despite the obvious pressure (financial and otherwise) that his mum was under, she didn't share the stress with her kids.

As a young child, Tom didn't know any different. All his friends had been dealt the same hand; he wasn't really aware there were people who had more access to money. While there were no trips to the movies, there were trips to the beach and lots of footy in the park with his brother or friends. The family didn't have a car or a credit card. If you wanted something, you saved for it. There was satisfaction in filling the money box and feeling its weight. Tom's impression of money was very practical—that you should save as much as you can—and he has continued this savings habit.

More than 25 years on, Tom's humble upbringing continues to influence his attitude to money. To this day he buys second hand, does plenty of research and looks for the best deal. Tom is conscious of having a safety net to fall back on. Tom is also happy to enjoy life and feels lucky to have means to give more to his kids than he had. He is somewhat cynical and cautious, and thinks people who don't like coffee are lucky! His mum will still travel halfway across Sydney on the bus to save a few dollars.

Some would say that Tom's upbringing influenced his spenditude for the better. He's a saver. For Tom, money is at the forefront of his mind—he continually seeks value in everything, from coffee to higher cost purchases. In some ways, money is a controlling factor in his life. However, Tom makes spending decisions in an automatic way: he has an automatic default on purchase decisions…'Where will I pay for this from?', 'Can I get a discount?', 'Is it tax deductible?', 'Can I wait until the next model?'

* * *

So, have you identified your type? Are you a Spender who's having fun, a Slender who gets anxious and frustrated about money or a Defender who has a plan and hates waste? You may feel you're a hybrid or on the cusp. That's okay, as life events can push you across types. No matter what spenditude you have now, the key is what you want to be in the future. For many, it's embracing the habits of a Defender.

See if you can identify your partner (if you have one) or family members, kids or parent's profiles. This is important as it may just open your mind to why some people find it easier than others to be less stressed and on track with their financial position. It will also help to reveal why money can cause problems in relationships. (Remember Andrew at the restaurant? He wanted to share his spenditude with Lucy as he felt it was important for their relationship.) We explore relationships and money further in chapter 9.

Remember: your spenditude has nothing to do with your age, your stage in life or your income! It doesn't always relate to your upbringing or parental guidance either.

My spenditude is . . .

My partner's/loved one's spenditude is . . .

Towards the close of each chapter we want you to check in to see if you've created a New Reality. A New Reality is defined as changing what's within and your external world reflecting it.

Okay, now that you've (hopefully) identified which category of spenditude you fit into, let's look at the importance of the most beneficial thing you can do in the bedroom ... that's right, we're going to examine the value of a good night's sleep!

Awareness:
I understand my current spenditude so I can see what needs changing.

Chapter 2

Dozy, sleepy, drowsy and weary

There are only two things that are satisfying in bed, and one of them is sleep. Sleep is the new black. It's a cool subject that has a direct link to wellbeing. Large organisations have identified that their employees perform well above average if they sleep well. Some employers even track their key people's sleep patterns to ensure they can extract the best return. Even sporting teams are linking sleep to on-field performance.

So it will come as no surprise that sleep is a key strategy in changing attitudes, behaviour and habits. In fact, it may well be the silver bullet. As for your spenditude, we have evidence that if you get a good night's sleep you're on your way to a far more positive spenditude.

And it's free and available every night in a bed near you!

Train your brain

One of the keys to habit change is to basically trick your brain. By improving your cognitive ability you can prepare your brain to accept habit change and stick with it, so it becomes your new normal. It's not difficult, but it does require a leap of faith.

To start moving some of your money habits, keep the end game in mind. Changing money habits will provide you with what you want: more choices, peace of mind and some form of financial security. These are excellent reasons to embark on behaviour change. So is having a healthy life.

Sleep: the brain changer

The first step to changing the way your brain thinks is to focus on your sleep. Yes, good old sleep. There's compelling evidence that we make better decisions, are more focused and feel better if we place more importance and focus on sleep. Numerous studies have linked inadequate sleep to depression, anxiety, repetitive thinking, memory deficit, ADHD and poor self-regulation. Yet, according to a 2016 survey by the Sleep Health Foundation, up to 45 per cent of adults report having insufficient sleep.

We asked Mark...

We asked Dr Mark Ryan—a psychiatrist and accredited neurofeedback practitioner who focuses on the mind-brain-body links—if he believes there could be a link between sleep behaviour and money-related behaviour.

His approach to supporting clients is to combine his understanding of insomnia and its role in mental health with leading-edge technologies and evidence-based research.

Mark has a particular interest in the link between sleep and both physical and psychological wellbeing.

His response is great news:

> Improve your sleep for better quality and more adequate duration of sleep, and you create a context for much better functioning in all areas of life — better mood and behavioural self-regulation; smarter money decisions; more skilful and better social, occupational and sporting performance and functioning.
>
> Sort out your sleep and you are on your way to sorting out your money habits.

Simple as that.

Sleep really matters

Adults are pretty good at prioritising things other than sleep: 'I'll just finish writing this email', I'm almost at the end of the movie', and so on. We feel signs of tiredness, but we think we have more in the tank we can push through.

In kids, the tired signs are clear: inattention, lashing out, tantrums, yawning and eye rubbing. But as adults we're less aware of the signals, particularly in ourselves. We overcome tiredness with another coffee or think we can 'catch up' on the weekend. Signs of tiredness in adults may be reactive or impulsive behaviours, not being as organised or having less focus. Scrambled thoughts and poor decision making are also issues for those of us who are sleep deprived, but the problem is that we have little awareness or insight into how impaired we really are.

Sleep is as important to our health as diet, exercise and general hygiene. Many important physiological functions are restored and re-set during sleep and there are strong links between sleep and illness, particularly mental illness (people with insomnia are more likely to experience depression). Sleep helps your body reset blood pressure, so there are links between sleep and cardiovascular disease as well as diabetes.

Sleep affects behaviour and helps us screen out irrelevant stimuli. Regardless of whether you think you're getting enough sleep, it's worth considering your nightly habits to see if there's room for improvement.

Mark explains...

> People who consistently get less sleep than their body requires don't notice their energy is lower overall. If you are sleeping six hours or less every night, you are in fact as cognitively and behaviourally disabled as if you have not slept at all for 48 hours. So you are basically drunk in terms of your brain function. But you don't have the physical symptoms that you would if you were drunk (stumbling or falling, for example) so you have no insight or awareness.

> Ultimately, sleep and our circadian rhythms are important to brain activity, hormone production, immune functioning and cell regeneration. There are quite a lot of essential things going on in our sleep. When we sleep better for long enough and get all the phases of sleep, we synchronise our biological rhythms and match them to social and other demands of life.

Get your nest ready

Sleep behaviours such as slowing down at night and relaxing are important and are equivalent to a pet dog or cat preparing its 'nest' before settling down to sleep. We can't be like the Eveready battery bunny...always switched on.

Think of your body as having a sleep–wake switch. Historically, when the sun went down, our bodies recognised the changes in light and triggered the switch. The same thing would happen in the morning when the sun rose. This is your circadian rhythm—your natural body clock. But our modern lives, particularly in the city, deprive us of those triggers in the natural environment. Matthew Walker (a scientist and professor of Neuroscience and Psychology) describes our urban environment and lifestyle as being 'dark deprived'.

Taking time to wind down at the end of the day is important. If we don't factor in some down time, both throughout the day and in the evening, the vigilance regulation system (which keeps us alert when we need to be) won't adequately synchronise with the circadian system. This affects our ability to fall asleep and to stay asleep, as well as the quality of our sleep, compromising sleep consolidation.

Many people skimp on sleep because they work late, get up early and restrict their sleep opportunity at both ends of the night. We need to prioritise sleep and give ourselves a chance to get enough.

The four phases of sleep

There's still a lot that we don't know about sleep. But we do know that there are four phases—these are the different stages that your body and your brain go through when you're asleep. Three of these belong to non-REM (rapid eye movement) sleep and one is REM sleep.

- The first stage is that state between being awake and asleep—it's when you sometimes get jerks of movement. It's quite easy to wake someone during this stage.
- In the second stage it's harder to wake someone as the brain has inhibited certain cognitive processes, such as hearing, so we're less affected by noise.

- The third stage is slow-wave sleep, or deep sleep. This is when some people walk or talk in their sleep. It's also when your blood pressure drops and your body has a chance to reset. Memory consolidation happens in slow-wave sleep.

- The fourth phase is REM sleep, where your eyes are moving rapidly beneath your eyelids but the majority of your other muscles are virtually paralysed. This is a dreaming state and your brain is very active. If you wake someone in REM sleep they're more likely to remember their dreams. Further memory integration and learning occurs in REM sleep and emotional processing and integration occur over the course of the night with each successive REM sleep stage.

We cycle through the four phases, often for about 90 minutes, but not necessarily in this order. All four stages are important to the restoration of your body.

Mark explains ...

There are three uncoupled processes involved in sleep and they need to be synchronised for sleep and wake to adequately occur.

Firstly, there is an accumulating sleep pressure. Slow waves accumulate in the brain over the time of being awake and using our brains (this is called process S). We want this to peak around the time we go to bed; hence long naps in the latter part of the day, caffeine and other stimulants (especially if taken in the latter part of the day) will disrupt this process. Sleep dissipates this sleep pressure.

Then there is the circadian rhythm (process C). Here we want social time and biological time to be about the same. This is easily misaligned when our social demands and failure to understand the environmental triggers such as blue light result in social time and biological time no longer coinciding.

Regularly needing an alarm clock is an indication that there is a misalignment and we are socially 'jetlagged'.

Finally, there is the vigilance arousal regulation system that needs to switch off, so the biological processes 'switch gear' to facilitate the circadian sleep processes and then switch on to enable wake up and adequate arousal/activation to support functioning throughout the day.

Like making good money decisions, there are a lot of relevant variables that need to be integrated to enhance the best outcome.

Sleep disruption and your health

By going to sleep later we're encroaching on slow-wave sleep, which is our deepest sleep and when our body has a chance to reset. When we've been using blue-light-emitting appliances late into the evening, we're likely to fall asleep because of sleep pressure, which is a build-up of the feeling of tiredness. After we've been in the dark for a while, our circadian sleep cycle switches on, which means the amount of actual restorative sleep we're getting is less than we think. It's worth noting that having a television on in the bedroom, or falling asleep with the lights on, can also dampen melatonin release — and therefore circadian rhythm sleep — because blue light penetrates closed eyelids.

During slow-wave sleep, certain proteins are removed from the brain. Not getting enough sleep means these proteins accumulate and this is associated with brain cell and network dysfunctions. There is emerging data about the relationship between adequate sleep — especially slow-wave sleep — and dementia and cognitive decline of ageing in vulnerable people.

What a good night's sleep can do for you

According to neuroCare, here are just a few of sleep's benefits.

Helps our memory

Lack of sleep affects our long-term and short-term memories. During sleep our body is able to process memories.

Prevents mood swings

Overemotional feelings and moodiness is linked to sleep deprivation. Long-term sleep deprivation can lead to anxiety and depression.

Restores and repairs

The hormones produced in sleep help to repair cells. Without sleep there are not enough cells to repair the body leading to a weakend immune system.

What a sleepy brain looks like...

When we do EEG recordings of people with Depression or ADHD, we often find 'beta spindles' in daytime brain activity which indicate 'sleepiness'.

Helps our concentration

Our motivation and energy is reduced when we have not slept enough the night before.

Happier relationships

Lack of sleep makes us less likely to pick up on the feelings of others around us and respond appropriately. It can also reduce intimacy with a partner.

Improves behaviour

Lack of sleep in children often causes irritation, lashing out, boredom, lack of focus, learning difficulties.

Helps us learn

Sleep helps concentration and capacity to take in new information. While we sleep the brain processes and problem-solves the information we have learned that day.

People who are chronic sleep restrictors (i.e. they consistently get too little sleep) are more likely to develop coronary artery disease and hypertension; have a stroke; become overweight or obese; develop diabetes; or get common cancers. Overall, this group has a higher all-cause mortality.

Sleep deprivation is bad for your health, but it's also not good for your financial position. A 2017 international study, 'The economic costs of insufficient sleep' by RAND Europe, confirmed that sleep deprivation is linked to poor financial outcomes and poor workplace productivity. Getting more sleep can improve your cognitive ability and therefore help you make better decisions with your money.

Simple steps to a good night's sleep

Here are Mark's simple steps for good sleep hygiene.

Booze

Many people believe alcohol helps them fall asleep. The truth is that the alcohol level in your blood can start to fall once you're asleep, causing a stimulant or wake-up effect, and alcohol consumption (at almost any level) can disrupt sleep (especially REM sleep). Alcohol can also cause fragmentation of sleep, affecting total sleep time, the time required to fall asleep and changed patterns of sleep.

In reducing your REM sleep, alcohol can also affect your memory and emotional regulation.

So, ideally, you should stay off the booze. If you don't feel you can in the long term, try to stay off it while you start your sleep hygiene routine so you can see the results. If you really can't stay away from it, try to restrict consumption so you finish at least 3 to 4 hours before you head to bed.

Eating, caffeine and exercise

Eating, drinking caffeine and exercising too close to bed time can affect your body's natural rhythms.

You don't have to eliminate coffee altogether, but try to restrict your caffeine intake to the morning because, when taken later in the day and in the evening, it can affect sleep onset and slow-wave sleep. Coffee, tea, cola and other soft drinks, as well as chocolate, all contain caffeine, which can make it harder for your body to fall asleep.

Eating close to bedtime can affect digestion and cause sleep interruptions, so try to finish your evening meal—which is often the biggest meal of the day—a couple of hours before bed.

Exercise is great for improving your sleep, but stick to exercising in the morning or early afternoon to ensure your sleep isn't affected. Exercising late in the day, especially within several hours of bedtime, will disrupt sleep as your physiological arousal will still be elevated at a time when it should be diminishing to facilitate the circadian rhythm.

Sex is a different beast—unless you have idiosyncratic sexual habits that might generate fear and danger or require hyper-athleticism (and therefore a high level of exercise intensity). For most people, sex facilitates relaxation and falling asleep.

Routine

Your body gets used to falling asleep at a certain time so a routine, with room for a bit of adjustment, is important for good health. Part of Mark's suggested sleep behaviours is to establish a routine of down time in the evenings for an hour or more before you go to bed. Create an environment that's conducive to winding down, including having a shower a couple of hours before bed to lower your blood pressure — and get the whole household in on the routine!

If you have to nap during the day, limit it to no more than 30 minutes. There's a device called the Thim, which tracks sleep and can help train you to have 10-minute power naps. Sleeping for longer during the day can make it harder to fall asleep at night.

On weekends it's okay to sleep in, but keep it to no more than 90 minutes after your regular wake-up time. If you find that most weekends you need to sleep beyond that, you're probably socially jetlagged and not getting adequate sleep during the week. This should be a prompt to review your sleep and other habits.

Blue light

In the evening our eyes need to avoid blue light to give our bodies the signal that it's night time—that is, sleep time. Blue light can boost mood, reaction times and attention: it's great in the daytime, but the opposite of what we need for sleep. The shorter wavelengths in blue light cause the body to produce less melatonin, which is essential for sleep. So reduce screen time in the evenings — dim screens to warmer colours or wear blue-light-blocking glasses.

Blue-light exposure in the morning helps calibrate the body's internal 'circadian' clock — this is the light that the body more naturally needs in the daytime. Phones, tablets, laptops and computers all emit high-spectrum blue light. This means that some time outside without sunglasses in the morning and perhaps again around midday will provide the best stimulus to synchronise and entrain the biological clock and social time.

If you can't do without screens in the evening, dim them to warmer colours. Check the settings in your phone: there may be a blue-light filter function that will help reduce blue light and can be set to come on automatically at a certain time. Wearing blue-light-blocking glasses is also a fabulous strategy that allows you to continue to use your screens — and to pretend you're a celebrity like Bono at the same time! Cheaper options are orange-tinted glasses, which block blue light. More expensive versions that appear clear but block blue light are also available. You'll find that the glasses actually help you drift off to sleep.

There are also programs available that alter the blue light on your computer screen according to the time of day; for example, f.lux (justgetflux.com) and Iris (iristech.co).

Other tips are to consider using warmer spectrum lights in your home and avoid fluorescent and LED lighting at night. 'Low blue' bulbs are available from a range of sources, including blockbluelight.com.au

It's okay to look at screens until you go to sleep if you're wearing blue-light-blocking glasses. But be aware that there's still a (lesser) effect on delaying and dampening the release of melatonin. If you wake in the night and want to look at a screen, use the glasses again.

Other sleep hygiene

There are lots of other good sleep hygiene habits you can try. For example:

- keep your bedroom dark, cool and quiet—wear an eye mask if need be
- sleep in a bed (not on the couch)
- keep your workspace away from your bed
- listen to a relaxing meditation or music
- avoid looking at the clock
- as we've mentioned already, it's okay to have sex as it acts as a great way to fall into a deep sleep (hopefully not during the act though!)

And remember, medicated sleep is not the same as natural sleep.

Paul's note:

Well, that sounds like a lot to take in. However, it's quite simple and it does work. I've improved my sleep hygiene over the past six months and I've seen the results. It's amazing how much better I sleep.

Janine's note:

Sleep hygiene is great, but I have young kids and even if they have a good bedtime routine (dinner, bath, teeth, books, sleep) they can still wake me up at night, which affects their sleep and mine. The internet is filled with stories of the weird behaviour of sleep-deprived parents! I have fallen asleep on many a train and missed my stop (on the way to work as well as home). I have rocked the supermarket trolley as though it was a stroller, called colleagues by my children's names and completely forgotten about meetings—all of which I credit to a lack of sleep. It completely messes with you.

Mark suggests keeping on top of the routine and using blue-light glasses—for both myself and the kids—for a couple of hours before bed, as well as sticking to some of the other sleep-hygiene rules mentioned above. With time, kids get older and sleep better. (Did you know that kids today sleep 75 minutes less than they did 100 years ago?) One of the main factors with kids is to ensure they are getting enough sleep. Sleep promotes sleep and keeping your kids awake actually makes things worse. So choose the argument, but don't negotiate sleep. Obviously, all parents would love to get their kids to bed quickly and easily, but that won't always be the case. Keep trying.

On the point of women, kids and sleep, there can be links between post-natal depression and sleep deprivation—but this is sometimes hard to resolve when your baby is awake all night. One thing new mothers can do is stay away from blue light (television, phone, etc.) when they are feeding bub overnight. It can stimulate both mum and bub, which is not great for anyone's sleep.

You can also check out light bulbs that will help at blockbluelight.com.au.

Sleepy teenagers

The earlier you go to sleep, the higher the likelihood that you'll get enough good-quality sleep. One measure of good sleep behaviours and sleep adequacy is noting the extent to which you need an alarm to wake up and how refreshed and alert you feel over the course of the morning (in particular).

If teenagers are on a screen very late into the night, it will cause sleep disturbance, which undermines their ability to make sensible decisions. As we mentioned earlier, blue-light-blocking glasses will help them to fall asleep more quickly. We tend to put rituals and routines in place for younger kids, but we're less likely to do this for ourselves and our older kids. Preparing the brain for sleep is important, so encouraging and demonstrating some of the prep behaviours is a good idea. Try to eliminate some of the bad habits: late to bed, too active too late in the evening, too much stimulation (television, social media, gaming, exercise).

Sleep affects behaviour. Parents know this. Teenagers, in particular, need to be careful of their social media engagement. But all kids are different and some have more self-discipline than others as well as individual variations in biology, physiology and learning histories.

Mark explains ...

> Lack of sleep leads to many behavioural issues and will cause teenagers to be quite inattentive and out of focus. It can also impact mental health conditions, particularly if they have a predisposition.

Shift workers and sleep

If your work is on a different schedule, you may have less control over setting a sleep routine. Shift workers such as international cabin crew and pilots, doctors and other health-care personnel are especially at risk—even more so when shifts rotate over the 24-hour timespan. This results in severe social jetlag because of the frequent variation in their sleep–wake cycle. As a result, these people are at increased risk of all the health problems outlined so far—and of course this is critical in terms of not only their wellbeing and health but also their occupational role performance and functioning.

Education and strategies are important. Workplaces must take a more informed approach to rostering, allowing circadian rhythms to be reset with adequate recovery time. Recovery 'power naps' are one way of helping shift workers adjust to their changing routines. Sleep hygiene is especially important for shift workers.

Obviously this is logistically a difficult problem and may require different solutions for each workplace.

Structural workplace changes and adjustments informed by the prevailing knowledge about sleep and social jetlag are necessary if these workers' health and work performance — as well as the wellbeing and safety of the general public — are to be adequately protected.

Money and sleep

If you can improve your sleep, you'll have set your brain for some habit-changing activity.

Here are some of the benefits of good sleep habits:

- You'll take in more information and be more inclined to act and stick to your new habits.
- Sleep helps reduce impulsiveness and enhances focus.
- Sleep can improve learning, decision making and emotional regulation (whereas lack of sleep affects our ability to 'read' others' emotions, learn routines and perform adequately).

If the frontal lobes of the brain haven't adequately 'woken up' (due to insomnia or sleep restriction), we see slower waves associated with sleep prominent in that brain region when we're in the awake state. This means 'executive' functions are impaired, which isn't good for making complex decisions about life and money matters.

When someone has addictive behaviour and sleep is considered as part of their recovery they're less likely to return to their addiction. So, improving sleep hygiene and sleep quality improves outcomes. Addiction is usually a situation where the priority, or value, is placed on something that's not ideal. While money habits don't always indicate addictive behaviour, if you can improve outcomes for addiction in general by addressing sleep, then it's not a far stretch that money habits can also be improved by addressing sleep.

If you're a Spender with poor sleep hygiene you won't move the dial on your behaviour.

If your spouse/partner is a Spender, don't blame them. Help them facilitate the discipline they need to improve their sleep as the first step.

No matter whether you're a Spender, a Slender or a Defender, sleep hygiene is a good way to re-focus as it gives your brain an opportunity to absorb and shift.

Tracking your sleep

Mark's final suggestion about sleep is that tracking your sleep is a great way to become more aware of how your sleep quality affects your life and what factors have an impact on sleep duration and quality. There are many sleep trackers on the market. Some are phone apps that use the microphone to detect sound and therefore movement. Some are wearables, such as a fitness tracker or a ring. You may start to see how your sleep habits equate to action and change in the rest of your life.

There is research that confirms that when we believe we have had a good night's sleep our cognitive function improves. So tracking your sleep quality may help.

Are you prepared to change the habit of a lifetime? It doesn't take much at all—just start with baby steps.

Want more?

For more information about Dr Mark Ryan, neuroCare, including research, technology and treatment, visit neurocareclinics.com.au.

If you're interested in reading more about sleep, Mark recommends these books:

Well Grounded: Neurobiology of Rational Decisions by Kelly Lambert

Why We Sleep by Matthew Walker

For blue light products check out blockbluelight.com.au

Next you're going to go on a journey revisiting your life. That's right—you're going to venture back through all the years you've lived and think about how the various signposts affected your beliefs about money.

Preparing the brain:

I'll start my good sleep hygiene so I can focus on my spenditude.

OVER TO YOU

Sleep-changer

For one month, try to go to bed at roughly the same time each night. Two hours before bed:

- Have a shower.
- Put on those blue-light glasses
- Avoid eating or drinking.

Just before going to bed:

- Make the room dark or wear an eye mask.
- Put your phone in another room.
- If you do read a screen in bed keep wearing the blue-light glasses. You'll drift off into a much better sleep.

After a month, it will be a habit.

Notice how sharp you are in the morning.

Chapter 3

Where did the time go?

As we journey through life, the years become like signposts on the side of the road on a long drive. They start to flick past in rapid succession. Birthdays start to merge in our memories.

We become aware of getting older, and for some that's a frightening experience.

Let's pause those signposts for a minute. Stop and think about where you are in your life journey. Imagine taking away the age issue and looking at life from a different perspective—perhaps that way you can get a better view of yourself and others around you who you care about.

Days of the week

Imagine your life in days of the week, with each decade being one day. Here's what your timeline would look like.

Monday

Monday is the formative years, up to age 19.

These are the years when we form our deep money values and motivators. Most of us have no idea how embedded these values are in our attitude to money. Our spenditude has been shaped by the end of Monday.

Tuesday

Tuesday is our twenties. At lunchtime on Tuesday you're 25. Some people are taking their first steps into the workforce while others might have been working since the end of Monday. Tuesday is when we see money coming into our bank account—or perhaps we don't see it, but we certainly spend it!

Defenders see Tuesday as their formative years. They set the platform by taking advantage of Einstein's eighth wonder of the world: money and time, the amazing power of compound interest. For Defenders money is growing and growing like a tumbleweed.

For Slenders Tuesday is the start of the travelator. It will take them to their destination, but not far beyond.

For Spenders Tuesday is the ticket to play. It opens up opportunities to spend their pay … and then some.

Wednesday

Wednesday is our thirties. This is when Slenders and Spenders may have their WTF moment. This is the moment when they say, 'Things will be okay—I'll just **W**ait **T**il **F**riday to sort them out.' This is a common mistake and of course completely misses Einstein's eighth wonder. So if you're currently a Wednesday, please consider the magic of time and money.

Defenders see Wednesday as their establishing decade. They may even wait to have kids later on Wednesday to ensure they're set up financially. The lure of having two incomes throughout Tuesday and Wednesday can be compelling—particularly if Einstein's eighth wonder is working for you (see chapter 6 for more about Einstein).

If it's currently late on Wednesday night for you, do you feel prepared for the weekend? Midway through our week we often have a shift in mindset: it's that moment in time when we have about the same amount of time ahead of us as behind us. This doesn't always lead to a mid-life crisis, but it can shift the way we think about our finances, friends and family as well as what we've achieved or want to achieve. When we're young, the future seems more infinite because most of us have more days ahead of us than behind us, giving us plenty of time to change.

Thursday

Thursday is our fabulous forties. Well, at least for some people. For others, it's a nightmare. Kids (if you have any) are sometimes older and possibly becoming more expensive to raise; FOMO may be driving decisions; and the real cost of living is challenging.

Thursday is incredibly reflective.

For Spenders each day in the week is the same as long as there's access to income. This means Thursday, for many Spenders, is still okay.

Slenders may feel less than fabulous; exhaustion from that treadmill is setting in. It's the frantic forties: trying to make sure they're sorting out the future, as well as keeping up with the cost of living, which seems to have increased at the same pace as their salary.

For Defenders Thursday can be a decade of consolidation — ensuring their path towards the weekend is sound and their assets are protected.

Thursday is also the day when our wonderful bodies can start to cost us more than before.

Friday

Friday. The day before the weekend. Our fifties.

Defenders plan to be in control on Friday, to make informed choices for the shape of their weekend.

Spenders find that the going is getting a bit tougher. They may be struggling to keep up their spending habits from earlier in the week. A redundancy or job change can bring them undone. This is definitely a door-closing day of the week.

Slenders are still pumping away on Friday and starting to realise they have no weekend plans. This can become a source of mental illness. Stress among Slenders on Friday is significant due to the realisation that the weekend is upon them and they don't have a good plan.

The weekend

Saturday and Sunday. Sixties and seventies. The weekend. Time to get some return on all the exertion during the week. Time to slow down and work smarter, or not work at all.

The weekends are problematic for so many of us. Do you know anyone who's really rocking their weekends? Those bloody Defenders are starting to cash in their chips from Einstein's eighth wonder and Slenders realise they may need to keep working well into Sunday. Meanwhile Spenders are struggling.

Next week

A new week and a long weekend. More and more of us will live into next week—Monday (eighties), Tuesday (nineties) and Wednesday (100s) and even beyond that.

According to data from the ABS (dated 2014 and 2015–2016) men born in Australia in 1960 had a life expectancy of around 68 years. They weren't expected to make it to Sunday! Women were expected to make it to Sunday lunch, with a life expectancy of 74 years.

These days it's over 80 and 84 respectively for men and women—everyone is hitting next week. We're living almost two full days longer than previous generations. This needs to be taken into account if you're a Spender or a Slender.

Defenders tend to have this stuff sorted during their first week.

STOP and reflect

Once you've identified your day and time, and that of those around you, consider what you're going to do next. Your options are:

A.   Nothing. Wait until tomorrow.

B.   Panic and then procrastinate and do nothing. Wait until tomorrow.

C.   Change your spenditude so you can enjoy your weekend. You deserve it.

You *can* recreate your week into a much healthier-looking weekend.

Remember that it's all about retraining your brain to think differently. Don't underestimate how flexible your brain can be. Give it a go.

In chapter 4 we get you to listen to that voice in your head that talks to you about money, and change some of what it says.

Life is too short:

I won't Wait Til Friday to plan my weekend.

OVER TO YOU

Did this chapter make you sit back and think hard?

A sample family's week

Here's a sample timeline with a family plotted onto it. How does this compare with your family?

In our sample family, there's 'Me', a Slender. There's only one Defender in the family and that's 'my' young son—and he's probably too young to really know if he's a true Defender.

There's definitely a family money culture that could be broken if 'Me' takes the first step.

Imagine being able to break this cycle and create some Defender behaviours. It would be a gift to your family, and in particular your kids.

My family's week

Describe your family and loved ones using the days of the week and then overlay their spenditude.

Try using the timeline to plot your family onto the week.

There you have it! A helicopter view of your family and loved ones.

This now gives you a picture of trends in spenditudes. It provides you with a chance to see what you're dealing with and it's a great starting point for identifying your—and your family's—spenditude.

Chapter 4

The voice inside my head

We all have a little voice in our head. It tells us all sorts of things that are often just a repeat of yesterday's voice. Do you believe you can train that voice to have a different narrative? If you could, would you listen?

Voices are your internal director—they keep you on track. For example, a voice in the morning wakes you up saying, 'Get out of bed; it's time to go have that jog'; another voice debates that opinion with, 'The bed is warm and I jogged yesterday'. Competing voices in your head address decision points throughout your day. Fleeting moments that can be more of a feeling than a formal thought.

But you can change your narrative.

A child safety group decided to change a narrative that we've all heard or used with kids: 'Don't talk to strangers if you're lost.' The group felt that if a child is lost, then everyone's a stranger. So the narrative was changed to, 'If you're lost, find a mum with kids and tell them you're lost'. This is a very simple example of changing a narrative to create better outcomes.

Money narratives

What about your money narrative? It also has competing voices and in some cases money is more challenging than other topics: 'Don't even think of buying that!'; 'Oh, that looks really tempting';'I deserve it'; or'Oh sh*t, I just bought that.' Just as in the children's narrative example above, by becoming aware of and changing your internal narrative towards money you can achieve better outcomes.

Your money narrative is something you believe even when there's no-one around. It's what you say to yourself about what you deserve in life. In identifying this narrative you're more able to decide if it serves you and to explore ways to change it. It will also bring you more confidence to avoid FOMO and social demands.

We all have old money songs playing in our head — narratives that we developed — and generally we don't ask our brain to change these. They're like old, worn, comfy shoes that you can't bring yourself to replace or give away.

Acknowledging your past and present behaviours with money will help you create change, build freedom and gain fulfilment (and replace the money songs playing in your head). The influences of your childhood, your culture and your peers are all significant. Do you have a sibling who has very different money behaviours from you? Same upbringing, different spenditude? Your narrative is influenced by your DNA and your environment. Often the way we perceive things, even in the same house, can differ.

For example, consider three siblings who grew up together: one has memories of having been 'poor' (she never got the brand-name clothing she wanted). The second believes they were 'cautious' with money (but they didn't miss out on anything). The third remembers a 'normal' childhood

('We were pretty lucky and had a few extras like a VCR and a computer'). Three different perceptions and narratives in one home.

Changing your tune

What feelings do you have towards money and your financial situation?

Here are some examples of old sound tracks:

- I would rather talk about sex, drugs or rock'n'roll than money.
- Wealthy people are all selfish.
- Money isn't everything.
- People who focus on money are ...
- I can't take it with me.
- I hate wasting money ... it drives me crazy.
- I always need at least $XX in my bank account, otherwise I freak out.
- Money is the root of all evil.
- I need to win the lottery kinda soon.
- I'm so guilty. I just spent the kids' holiday money on a night out.
- I always set myself a money goal and get quite pissed off if I don't achieve it.
- The biggest barrier to living my best life is money.

Here's the changed narrative — the new sound tracks:

- I love to invest in experiences, not assets.
- I work for purpose and I hate waste.
- I don't need much.

- Money doesn't define me.
- I'm always going to be okay if I stick to my plan.
- I love being in the black. It's liberating.
- I'm encouraging my brain not to listen to my old money soundtrack.

So, how much does our money narrative drive our financial outcomes?

The answer is *a lot*.

Whether you're a Spender, Slender or Defender, thinking about your reactions to financial issues will guide you towards beginning to reveal some of your core beliefs. Your story. Your narrative. Your feelings and responses to money.

For kids, a key way of learning is through observation. Our perceptions are more important than anything else. What money behaviours did you see on a day-to-day basis during your childhood? Frugal? Big spender? Never enough? Could Mum only buy something with Dad's permission (or vice versa)? Did they document all the bills with high levels of stress, knowing exactly what they spent? Was money a subject that regularly caused fights? Did something big happen that changed your family's financial position (for better or for worse)?

We receive our first lessons about money way before we go to school and certainly a long time before we receive our first pay cheque. It's true that the financial choices your parents make, and that you experience in your childhood, have a huge influence on your spenditude as an adult. But this doesn't mean you'll necessarily replicate their behaviour—in fact, many of us go the other way. The most important factor to consider is how we perceived money in our childhood, and this may differ between children in the same family.

A 2013 University of Cambridge study by David Whitebread and Sue Bingham suggested that money habits are formed before the age of seven. Another study based on psychologist Walter Mischel's 'marshmallow test' showed that in homes where money is tight, parents are more likely to give in to kids' demands and kids are less able to learn about delayed gratification. However, the behaviours you observed in childhood are only part of your story and your experiences. (Also, don't place too much blame on your parents; they formed their own habits through their life experience.) More about kids and money in chapter 9.

The process of finding out why money is important to you and why you make certain choices is an essential step towards digging deeper into your personal money story and changing your narrative.

What's your story?

What's money to you?

...the root of all evil; important; power; energy; not everything; achievement; bad; status; unimportant; anxiety; addictive; a gift; complicated; guilt; success; independence; opportunity...

A tale of three

Three friends. All are similar in age with similar circumstances—women who work, have kids and are married.

Claire goes shopping in her lunch break and loves to buy a new pair of shoes. She leaves them at work and wears them many, many times, before she takes them home. Why? So she can legitimately say to her partner, 'Oh these? No, I've had these for ages.'

Amy also loves to shop, but she's much more open about it. She receives parcels in the mail and the delivery person knows the house well! In fact, her partner buys things too and neither of them objects.

Nicole isn't a shopper, but she does buy things online sometimes. When she does she's careful to research, look for the best deal and make sure shipping is free. She'll plan purchases and wait for a sale. Nicole will join a mailing list for a product she needs, but remove herself from that list once the purchase has been made. Nicole sometimes feels guilty about spending and is careful to tell her husband (or is she really telling herself?) that the online store has free delivery and free returns. Her husband doesn't care if she buys something. He knows she's good with money.

What creates these behaviours and the differences in behaviour? Without diving too deeply into the particulars of each person (and relationship), where did these spending habits come from? Claire is a Spender who is married to a Defender. She grew up in a single-parent home where money was tight. Now she struggles to resist the instant gratification of buying. Claire feels she missed out on a lot as a child and this results in wanting to have a better lifestyle and the look of success. She earns and she spends. Yet she's compelled to hide her spending. Her narrative of not wanting to miss out, is contrasted against a sense of guilt. Ultimately, she believes she missed out on a lot and she doesn't want to feel like that anymore.

Amy and her partner are both Spenders. They have similar behaviours and are therefore more able to be open about them. Both value lifestyle highly; they want to enjoy life. They eat out, travel, shop and manage their money with a sense of optimism. Amy grew up in a home where money was available, but budgeted carefully. Amy's mum stayed at home with the kids and her dad controlled the finances.

Amy believes her mum missed out on a lot as a result of not having access to extra money when she needed it (without having to ask her dad). She'll never put herself in a position where someone else controls her spending, and so she buys whatever she wants.

Nicole is a Defender married to a Slender. Her sense of planning, focus and justification for her purchases is clear. Nicole grew up with two hard-working parents who never seemed to make ends meet, causing many an argument. She's money savvy, frugal and has an understanding of her financial situation. She applies a value lens (remember this term from chapter 1?) to all her purchases. Nicole has a real need for financial security. The tense environment in her childhood around money and the sense of never knowing if they had enough drives her choices as an adult. Her husband is a Slender who thinks she can be a bit too focused on money at times.

When thoughts become things

When things happen in our life, we respond to them with thoughts and feelings, and this is manifested in our behaviour. If you believe you 'never win anything', then you probably don't. If you believe you're destined to remain in your financial situation, then things are unlikely to change. There's a voice in your mind that has lots of associations to money, both positive and negative. It's easy to get caught in the old routine or money song if you don't identify the lyrics. The action you take as a result of that mental story really cements the beliefs. It's not only about childhood, but about work, relationships and what you believe you deserve.

Consider your situation, events that have occurred through-out your life and your responses to these events.

A Spender and a lump sum are soon parted

If you're not overly wealthy, then you've probably at one point or another daydreamed about a lottery win and having loads of spare cash. What would you do with it—have holidays, improve your lifestyle, be generous? It's a fun game to play. Even with a win like this, you still see yourself as being the same person, just with a bigger bank balance. People often feel that having more money would enable them to re-focus without the restrictions that come with everyday life and earning money—that money would bring freedom. However, a shift in your financial position (for better or worse) doesn't change your personal money narrative—that is, your personal truth.

If your money narrative is all about not missing out and being generous, then a lottery win could cause havoc. There are many stories of lottery winners who put themselves in a worse position 12 months on from their win. The data suggests that lottery winners are more likely to declare bankruptcy than the average person. They can struggle with mental health as well as being more likely to divorce.

The same concept goes for retirees. Most of us have no skill in managing a lump sum. It seems to fall through our fingers quite quickly. Spender retirees tend to move to government support before they know it.

As with the lottery winners and retirees, money, over a period of time, is an illusion that requires perspective.

Stimulus and response

The world projects its demands onto us from every angle: social media, advertisements, television, movies … the list is seemingly endless. So how do you find contentment and 'enough' among the noise and the hype? The feelings that this noise creates are often ones of shame, anger, anxiety or jealousy. But what we observe is more of a social mask than reality.

Two quotes from the popular sage Dr Phil McGraw, of daytime television fame, come to mind: 'We compare our personal truth to everyone else's social mask' and 'If we think we are second class, we will generate results that a second class person deserves'.

The closer you are to understanding your own money narrative, the more easily you're able to ignore and avoid the noise. You become less susceptible to the triggers that will influence your decisions.

Human behaviour is often automatic. Are all our actions actually choices? Walking past someone busking or begging on the street requires a decision: to give or not. Similarly, a more formal donation to a charity is a choice. Does this decision come back to your financial position or your money narrative? There's certainly an overlap.

'I can't afford to donate.'

'I want to donate but don't want to over-extend myself.'

'I work hard for my money.'

'Charity begins at home.'

'I'll donate once I'm financially secure.'

Your money narrative—the voice in your head—affects the more automatic behaviours and the formal decisions. Whether your financial behaviour is about shopping, spending or the opposite (hoarding, fear of loss, insecurity) there are emotions and a story attached.

If it's simply that you want to save more and spend less, you may find some use in unsubscribing from emails/follows/likes. The temptation to spend can be reduced by removing some of the marketing we're bombarded with every day on social media (by the way, this is a good idea). However, if you're not addressing the underlying narrative and considering how that narrative serves you, there's unlikely to be any long-term change.

Narratives come in many forms. Getting a good deal might give you a sense of winning, of feeding your competitive spirit. Shopping might be a leisure activity, one that brings a sense of satisfaction or even joy. Perhaps it's a more negative story or feeling, a fear of losing money that means you effectively hoard it. Maybe you have difficulty making a decision for fear of making the wrong one, never having confidence in your ability to manage your money.

Breaking the poverty cycle

It's hard to imagine being born into, and living in, extreme poverty, yet the World Bank estimates that around 10 per cent of the global population lives on less than $2 a day. If you couldn't read and write well, and couldn't sign your name, would you be able to access a bank account? Would you believe that, like generations before you, this is just the way it was?

Good Return is a small Australian not-for-profit organisation that works with people living in extreme poverty. Their goal is to end extreme poverty by 2030. Good Return focuses on reaching people with the least privilege and the greatest barriers. It works with an emphasis on women, because poverty does too.

Good Return's success comes as a result of education centred around behaviour change. Its training develops new skills and knowledge to help participants make choices that improve their overall wellbeing. Opportunity and empowerment help the poorest of the poor work their way out of poverty.

Good Return's programs enhance the knowledge, skills and behaviour of the communities they work in and enable people to change their lives and escape extreme poverty. Behaviour change and financial literacy is a game changer for people living on less than $2 a day.

For more information, visit goodreturn.org.au.

Disclosure: Paul is a proud ambassador for Good Return.

There's conflict in my head

Going back to our days of the week in chapter 3, you'll find that people in their 'next week' (80+) often talk about the house they 'shoulda' bought or how they 'coulda' saved more money and gone on more holidays or what they 'woulda' done differently. Coulda, shoulda and woulda are three sisters who need to be erased from our thinking. Coulda, Shoulda and Woulda will lead us to a place where we feel unfulfilled. Replace them with baby-step changes and you'll never have to visit them again.

When you're considering buying something—from a purchase that seems small and insignificant, such as a coffee, to a much larger purchase, such as a car or a home—there are forces competing in your brain. One part of your brain is seeking happiness: anticipation delivers a hit of dopamine. Another part of your brain is trying to keep you safe—to avoid risk. One of these will dominate based on what you're experiencing (I can smell the coffee; I deserve a coffee; I'm tired) and you'll make a choice accordingly. But after you purchase something, do you ever have a sense of regret? The other part of your brain takes over (I didn't really need it; I already had one; I've been trying to save more …). Buyer's remorse is a real thing—and Spenders, Slenders and Defenders can all experience it. These conflicting beliefs and attitudes are called *cognitive dissonance.*

The next phase of buyer's remorse is the rationalisation—you try to convince yourself that your purchase decision was the right thing to do. With a small purchase such as a coffee you can 'get over it' pretty quickly, but with larger purchases this can be harder. In an age of e-commerce, we can purchase almost anything from almost anywhere. The marketing we're exposed to builds on our FOMO. The sheer range of choice for any given item can compound our chance of regret so we're unsure if we made the right decision.

Our money narrative, combined with the pressure of marketing and our social network, can make us believe that acquiring an item will bring happiness. Our brain might back this up with both our money narrative and a hit of dopamine. 'If I just had this, life would be better.' The act of acquiring the item may bring a temporary sense of happiness, but it doesn't have a long-lasting effect.

The concept of cognitive dissonance is quite real in that we trade off our spenditude with our sense of doing the right thing. Is there a way to avoid the let down? Well, the research says that experiences (as opposed to acquiring objects/items) provide a smaller risk of buyer's regret because the memory and feelings that experiences create outlive the 'boost' that you receive when you purchase an item. There's still risk involved though. A psychological heuristic called the 'peak–end rule' suggests that we judge experiences by two things: (1) the peak moment—the most extreme part of the experience, be it good or bad—and (2) the end point.

Once again, your brain is kind of playing a trick on you. Consider a holiday that was great overall: everything went smoothly, the weather was perfect and you enjoyed yourself, except for two things. Halfway through the trip the key experience you had planned was cancelled due to something out of your control and then on the last day of the holiday you got sick. Overall, it was a great trip, but the peak experience was one of disappointment and the final moment was one of illness. As a result, your brain might bring on some of those feelings of buyer's remorse.

What will you do with this voice in your head?

A Spender narrative

Matthew is a Spender. He feels that life is way too short to worry about money … So he doesn't. He earns it and spends it. When there's none, Matthew goes out and earns some more—or, better still, he borrows what he needs. 'I will sort it out then,' he says of having to pay it back at a certain time.

Anyway, spending is fun. It provides Matthew with a well-earned sense of satisfaction. Perhaps he sometimes does get buyer's regret, but that's mainly due to the fact he probably feels guilty—but only if he's over-extended. But that goes away and on he goes.

Matthew loves technology: he has an uncontrollable urge to buy the latest. In particular phones. When Apple announces a date for the release of a new iPhone he feels the excitement build. Matthew will be near (or at) the front of that line at the Apple store. 'I can't wait.' The thought of getting home and opening that box, unwrapping all the exquisite packaging that Steve Jobs was so fussy about and then taking the shiny new phone out and plugging it in so it takes its first breath ... Of course, he buys the biggest and best version and the best plan as well. You know, the plan that allows an upgrade when the next model is launched. 'What does he do with the old phone?' we hear you say. Ha ... in truth it's not even two years old, and he probably gives it away to a friend. Not much good to him now. Matthew will always have the latest and greatest. 'Wow, did you see the quality of the photo?' he asks, as he snaps one straight out of the box.

(The iPhone mania is almost too powerful for many Spenders. Their lack of delayed gratification, no interest in cost and their desire to have it in their hands *now* is way too powerful. Of course, Defenders have a very different narrative.)

Spenders may feel that too much focus on money is wrong, and they can also be envious of others.

Are your associations to money all about stress or boredom or debt? Perhaps you feel that money is just something that flows through your hands and that wanting more of it is greedy or extravagant. Does it feel like you need to be paid more to survive and that causes you grief? Is your self-talk focused on pain and fear or perhaps just a sense that it will work itself out?

Does it worry you that you're not interested in money? You hate the B word (budgeting) and you find it easier just to close off and get on with your life.

Do you feel that if someone else tells you to read a book about 'better money management' you'll hit them over the head with your empty wallet? Is it possible that you're a Spender?

A Slender narrative

Alex is a Slender. He's trying hard to be a role model for his kids, but he also wants to have a good life. Alex abruptly stopped buying coffee after noticing how his habit had escalated and thinking about how much it was costing him. It lasted a while, but then he started feeling annoyed. After all, he works hard, and why shouldn't he be able to buy coffee? By his calculations he saved about $150 over the past month! Alex pays attention to his money, but he doesn't have a proper budget (who has the time?!). He looks for what's discounted when doing the grocery shopping and pays his bills on time.

Last weekend his son, Oliver, needed new football boots. Alex really wants to make sure his kids have the things they need. Without considering the cost, they visited the local shopping centre, got a great pair of boots, and while they were there picked up a few other gifts, a new footy and decided to have lunch while they were at it. Alex came home having had a good day. He didn't pay any attention to the fact that he'd spent around $400 in a few hours.

Alex doesn't understand why his bank balance doesn't ever seem to grow, despite the fact that he has really rationalised his coffee habit and never pays a late fee on a bill.

Another example is Mary. She drives her husband crazy by spending hours doing the grocery shopping, trying to get the best price on each item, meal planning and taking a list. But on the same day, Mary walks down the street and spends hundreds on a dress with no sense of bargaining or really considering the cost. This is the narrative of the Slender.

If you're a Slender, then perhaps you feel that hard work = deserving. Maybe you feel envious of others and jealous that they seem to have more than you. Or maybe you're resigned to the feeling that your mortgage controls your life. Alex and Mary are typical Slenders: frustrated that they're not moving forward. Trying hard to do the right things, but without focus.

Perhaps you're married to someone who spends too much when you're trying to save. Is money on the top of your list of concerns? Does it wake you up or, worse still, does it make it hard to sleep? Are you annoyed that you do all the right things but you don't seem to be getting anywhere with your finances? You feel like you're on a conveyor belt going nowhere.

Some people just seem to be better with money than others. Are you a Spender or a Slender renting and getting annoyed at that neighbour who seems to be doing so well and has two investment properties (even though you know they don't earn anywhere as much as you do)? Are they drug dealers or do they just approach money differently? Why does it seem effortless for some? Does it concern you that time is ticking by and you haven't accumulated enough assets? If this sounds familiar, then is it possible you're a Slender?

A Defender narrative

Jimmy is a Defender. He has a great feel for money and money has always been his thing. He doesn't mind spending, however he *hates* waste. He just can't do waste. His weak spot is his passion for golf. He loves his Saturday morning game and is very keen to use the best gear. How does his Defender radar work when his passion can be expensive and feeds into his feeling of satisfaction? Well, he does have all the gear and he does play when he travels. This is expensive, however his value lens is still working even though his passion for the sport does seduce him. Jimmy will buy the expensive clubs but not just to be satisfied, and certainly not to impress others.

Jimmy's formula is, 'I buy the best clubs so I can get as much benefit/performance as I can'. Jimmy's formula for spending is:

value = performance minus price over time.

Jimmy's purchases aren't short term. He'll try and get the best deal for the latest clubs, and make sure the price is right. Jimmy does the research to ensure he has the knowledge to make the best purchase decision. He uses his own money (never debt).

Meanwhile, the Spender is on the third hole by now with their new clubs shining in the sun and no real thought of performance minus price. It's just a different way of thinking.

Defenders are looking for the security and satisfaction that come with using their value lens. Defenders are generally confident with their financial affairs and are great at saving, and staying out of debt.

Defenders don't always enjoy the freedom that they could for two key reasons:

- They hate waste and are careful about spending, wanting to be confident in their decisions.
- They feel they're not satisfied with their financial situation: 'When is enough, enough?'

The art of storytelling

Outside your narrative there are forces that have created challenges for all of us. The way we communicate has changed forever and the art of storytelling (our original and best source of wisdom) has been bent out of shape.

The digital revolution that encompasses us has created a different form of storytelling:

- Tell me now.
- I can't wait.
- Tell me in bite-size grabs.
- One click or I'm out.

We tend to talk about sex, drugs and politics before we share our money wisdom. We don't pass down wisdom through stories and even if we did we've made money a taboo topic. What hope have we got?

Storytelling is the oxygen that passes down wisdom. It has been since time began. In Australia, the Indigenous community continues to share stories through over 60 000+ years of history—the oldest living culture on the planet, and one with primarily a spoken language of more than 250 language groups. Perhaps we should all be envious of this storytelling culture that remains alive.

What's your story? What have you observed through your childhood and your life experiences that has influenced the story in your head? What's your current narrative to money and when is a good time to change your narrative? (*Now*, of course.)

Brett's story

Almost all of Brett's childhood memories have some sense of money related to them. Money was absent. It was limited to the point of stress. Constantly.

Brett's dad worked two jobs: 18-hour days laying bricks and in the pub. His mum worked 18-hour days taking care

---

of three kids and trying to keep the 100-acre property running. It was the late 1980s; however, their property had no mains water or electricity and was about a 45-minute drive from the closest town. Cooking, heating and hot water all came through the wood-burning stove in a home that his dad was slowly building but never finished — mainly due to a lack of time and money.

When Brett was about eight he went to the local country show. All his friends were going on rides, having a good day out. He had been given 50 cents. A friend told him you could win money by riding a bull — as much as $15. He felt he had nothing to lose and plenty to gain so he strapped himself in and grabbed third place to win $5. It wasn't much, but it was enough to have a good day.

Money was a negative force in the home. It caused a lot of fighting and was certainly a factor in Brett's parents separating. Despite the financial difficulty, Brett relishes the memories of living on the land. His mum was clever, hard-working and resourceful. She grew most of their food, had chickens and preserved food when it was abundant. Because of his mum, no matter the financial situation, there was always something to eat. But the extras were harder to manage: education, fuel for the car and Brett's motorbike, which he used to get to school, gas for the fridge, building products and gifts required more money than the family had. Money was managed on a weekly basis and prioritised with need. The family would sometimes trade food with a neighbour who had better networks and could assist in trading for other items.

If there wasn't enough fuel for the generator, Brett's dad would siphon some from the car fuel tank. It was a pretty risky way of getting a mouth full of petrol, but there was

(continued)

Brett's story *(cont'd)*

sometimes no choice. At Christmas his mum would drive along the local roads looking for a good Christmas tree on the edge. She would drop Brett off with a hand saw to cut one down and come back after turning around to get it in the car as quickly as possible. All possible options to save money and be resourceful were taken. Despite their family's financial position, they always got a couple of Christmas gifts. Brett's mum wouldn't let them down. Brett always wondered how, but didn't ask.

When Brett was 16 he moved out of home to the city on a sport scholarship. Life was better in many ways. Accommodation was paid for; food was supplied. He received a government study allowance, which gave him spending money. Those couple of years made him feel wealthy and fortunate. A few times his parents asked him for money, but that was no problem.

After a couple of years things changed. Brett had to move out, find work, a place to live, pay the bills. The years of ease were gone. Not long after getting set up in his own place, a few friends invited him for a night out. Brett played the pokies and won. A few small and a few big wins later, it felt like an easier way to earn some more money than the hardship he had lived with for most of his life. Soon he was struggling to buy food and waiting for the next pay cheque. Some weeks he was really well off, happy and feeling successful. Others were embarrassing, depressing. Gambling took hold and lasted about 18 months before he noticed that the club was doing some big renovations and (excuse the pun) the penny dropped that he was helping to fund them.

Brett fell back on what he had learned as a child. He was working three, sometimes four jobs, studying at university and paying the bills. He was too busy to gamble and he started to see his finances turn around. He had a stash of cash and the visual helped — seeing it getting bigger. Keeping busy was a major factor in making the change.

As an adult, married, with children, Brett still thinks he's a little unpredictable with money. The lessons he learned in his childhood were to value and respect money, but also that money didn't buy happiness.

Despite the hard times, and the links to his parents' rocky relationship, he has fond and happy memories of living on the land and working hard with very little money.

In the same way that his mum was always able to find money for gifts, Brett considers himself to sometimes be too generous with others. At the same time, he looks for a bargain, always checks the sale rack and if in doubt won't spend.

With hindsight Brett believes that it's sad to recall the effect that money had on the family, over and above the hardship of living on the land.

The observations and experiences of Brett's childhood shaped associations between extraordinary levels of hard work and there never being enough to create a financial difference. While the hard work ethic has been instilled in him from a very young age, so has a sense that money is not something to place too much emphasis on — it leads to relationship issues and doesn't bring happiness. Brett finds it difficult to focus on money.

Brett is a Slender. Although he has been in situations where money is extremely tight, he doesn't display consistency or apply the value lens that a Defender has.

Brett's money narrative is mostly about security—there's comfort that can be gained from money, which is not to be taken for granted. However, he knows that there are ways to get by with very little, which brings with it a sense of optimism. He was, and continues to be, grateful for what he has, which means he finds it hard to prioritise finances.

There's conflict in Brett's money narrative—the sense that he's doing well and should be happy, giving generously, supporting others not doing as well contrasted with the knowledge that things can change quickly and he should make sure of his own security. Primarily, he finds it hard to think about gaining more wealth as he feels happy to have improved his lot in life.

A Spender named Anna (part 2)

You'll remember we met Anna in chapter 1. Anna grew up with handouts. Money was available and allowed for a life of partying. Lifestyle was key. She was surrounded by many friends who enjoyed her generosity. When her parents separated, Anna was in her mid twenties. The flow of money stopped. Suddenly. At Christmas time.

It was the steepest of learning curves. Left with credit card debt, no money management skills, an expensive lifestyle and a generous nature, Anna felt somewhat deserted. She had had access to unlimited funds—money that, she felt, was compensation for her parents not being around much.

Unfortunately, her mum also had no money-management skills. Anna and her mother had similar habits: 'Don't worry about the money or the spending. Dad will sort it out.' Age was on Anna's side in terms of being more willing to accept the change, but her mum was struggling. Where Anna was able to start dealing with the situation and move forward, her mum felt very lost: 'poor me'. They'd both not paid any attention to understanding money, and no-one was there to guide them.

Anna fell back to her ultimate motivator, which was that her family was more important than the money. This took priority. Anna was trying to get her own life under control while coaching, supporting and guiding her mum.

The impact of community was significant. Anna had witnessed the impact of a lack of money. Her extended family had shown much love, but a lack of money led to a lack of choice. In her wider community, teen pregnancy and unemployment were common: a victim mentality.

The contrast to her life so far—one of opportunity, travel and education—was significant.

Anna made the choice to leave.

The narrative that had been shaped through Anna's upbringing was one that could not equate love and money. Money was opportunity. To have no money was not a real option. While it might not bring love with it, it granted comfort and escape. Anna valued this comfort and opportunity and realised that this could not be taken for granted. Although she also valued the love and kindness that had come from her family, she felt that she could demonstrate a different way forward.

The door-closing moment of her parents' separation forced Anna to consider her relationship with money. The push and the pressure to find her own security helped Anna change her behaviours for the better.

Anna has experienced both sides of the money divide: her extended family with limited funds, and living as a Spender with abundant resources. Despite her spending ways, Anna's money narrative had to shift. Anna wants to bring change to her wider community. Her knowledge that things can change quickly—for better and for worse—has helped her build her own security.

More about Anna later …

Change the record:

I'll re-write my narrative so it's a positive voice inside my head.

Did any of chapter 4 trigger you?

How about doing a narrative stocktake?

Ever heard about the idea of writing things down and burning them to let go? Don't do that! Review the words you write and you'll have a sense of what you need to do—what needs to be forgotten, forgiven and let go of. What experiences do you need to learn from? Embrace the discomfort. You have choice in the way you respond to the memories and thoughts. Reflection may cause you to cringe or have a sense of loss/pain. *But* it will bring growth + wisdom + financial wellbeing. You have a choice in the way you move forward. Which life journey will these memories and thoughts direct you to?

Here are some examples of a money stocktake. Write a couple of words in response to each point below in the context of money. What values or feelings do you have about each one?

Finish the sentences...

- Financial independence is...
- I got paid yesterday and I...
- When I spend money I instantly...
- When money is tight I...
- I'm doing okay/well/badly financially because I...
- Looking at my bank account I feel...
- Money is for...
- My partner/kids are influenced by my money behaviour...
- What childhood memories have surfaced?

Money: how do you respond to the word? Is money your superhero? Are you waiting for it to come and save the day and treating it with reverence, respect and awe? Do you wish it would go away? When you think of money, does it bring to mind a person or place? Is it high on your list of personal values? Are you competitive with money?

What other life events have influenced your money relationship? Work through the list in the table below.

Work	Did you lose a job/not get a job? Were you refused a pay rise, or did you miss a bonus? Are you still angry, hurt, annoyed? How does this influence you today?
Relationships	Are you in a relationship with a Spender? Did you lose money as the result of a relationship breakdown? Do you earn more/less than your partner? Are you embarrassed by your story and do you hide it? Have you not forgiven yourself? Are you holding onto regret? Do you have a secret bank account?
Theft / Win	Did a sudden shift in your financial position remove any sense of control, change other people's relationships with you or provide an opportunity you didn't believe you deserved? Are you ashamed of your financial position, be it wealth or financial stress?
Moments	Did you have an awkward money moment(s)? Are you trying to keep up with the Joneses? Are there cultural norms or expectations?
Women	There are a whole other set of 'rules' that women impose on themselves (more in chapter 8) that influence their relationship with money. Do you rely on your partner (too much)? Are you annoyed that childcare or elder care falls to you?
Self-talk	Do you have a lot of negative self-talk about money and your potential? Do you feel frustrated that you don't know where your money is going? Are you in denial and do you avoid making choices because you anticipate that change will be difficult or painful?

Give yourself some time to complete your narrative stocktake.

Have you been able to start retraining your brain? If you've been able to take stock of the voices in your head, then you've benefited from reading this chapter. Congratulations! You have a sense of what you're feeling and thinking about money.

In chapter 5 we look below your money narratives and thoughts. What's under the surface? Why do you feel this way and what's the origin of your spenditude?

Chapter 5

The *why* factor

Mahatma Gandhi said, 'A man is but the product of his thoughts. What he thinks, he becomes.' Who are we to argue with Gandhi?

Have you ever wondered why we do what we do around money?

This is a fundamental question to any habit change. If you can't work out your *why*, then you may never be able to move forward. In dieting, the *why* factor is rarely 'I am always hungry'; it's more than likely an esteem issue or something that affected you when you were young. We know that those affected by any form of eating disorder generally trace the reason back to events in their (young) lives.

The same goes for money and our attitude or behaviour towards it.

'Shanelle is generous.' 'Bill's a tight-arse.' 'Franco is always worried about money.'

Although this is what people see, it's only part of your story. Think of an iceberg. You can only see 10 per cent of it above the water. What's on and above surface is only the visible part of your spenditude. The *why* makes up the 90 per cent below the watermark. It's deep-rooted in your past; it's your values, those deep influences that drive you and your needs—and it's often invisible to you. Your money narrative (from chapter 4) sits just at the water line, mostly out of sight, but you can hear the noise it creates.

In order to really change the 10 per cent above the surface you need to address the 90 per cent below.

what I feel
about money

Money
narrative

why I feel
like I do

Focus
Attitude
Life experience
Deep values
Family
culture

what
others see

The voice in
your head

Origin of your
Spenditude

Paul's dad — 75 years of Defending

My dad is 90. Dad is a proud man born between the two great wars and just before the Great Depression. He worked for the same employer for over 40 years and retired at 60. He has spent the past 30 years as a successful retiree.

I never really considered his spenditude because he always managed his finances and rarely discussed money.

Dad had a stroke last year and is losing some of his cognitive skills. This has changed everything for him. He can no longer read very well and he can't do his own paperwork — something he was very fussy about. Recently he and I had a conversation around his money as I am now looking after his bills and banking (BTW he is way better than me at this task). His world may be confusing; however, his core behaviour to money is unflinching. He wanted to know exactly where every dollar was in his bank accounts and in particular he wanted to know the balance in his working account. The reason he wanted to know is deeply embedded into his psyche. He told me, 'I was broke when I was younger and I never ever wanted to be in a position where I didn't have at least three months' pay in my bank account.' This is what he called his safety limit.

As it happened, his account had dropped below his 'safety limit'. He became agitated for the first time in months. All he wanted was to get the balance up to that limit. He told me he couldn't function if he didn't meet that threshold.

What I observed from this chat with Dad is that he has deep-rooted money values. They are over 75 years old and have served him well. In fact, he can't function without them.

I realised that my dear old dad has been a Defender all his life — and it ain't going to change any time soon.

What motivates you?

A 2018 survey by Australia's leading digital bank reported that 86 per cent of us don't know how much we spend each month and less than one-third use any kind of money-management tool.

There's an old saying that your bank statement and calendar don't lie. If you review them, you'll see what you're really doing with your time and money. This is how we dig to find the gold: the truth of where you're placing value.

Tracking your spending can bring clarity. What if your bank statements and calendar could reflect something you're proud of? Rather than tracking your money to restrict your spending and budget, can you use budgeting tools in a different way, simply to increase your awareness?

If your bank statement and calendar don't reflect the story that you want, where to from here?

In a world that's driven by consumerism, where success is defined by income and 'stuff', we're all too likely to align our job titles or postcode to our self-esteem and values. Research by UBank confirms that we're so influenced by 'likes' on social media that some of us spend just to get a positive response and some would even prefer these 'likes' to cash! When trying to make changes in our lives we often focus on the end game: the big goal, the big change. We may think that if we're patient and spend a little less, things will get better. Yes, that helps, but if you address some of the 90 per cent under the water, then you can make bigger leaps, more quickly. Habit changing is a difficult beast. It seems easy until you start. Then it can be hijacked by our daily lives and patterns. If it were easy we would all have perfectly brilliant habits. So we need to identify something that can give us the edge.

In looking at your bank account, don't judge yourself. The exercise is about evaluating: figuring out what's habit and what makes you happy. Your bank account and calendar can show you.

Comparing your motivators—*needs, drivers* and *values*—to your time and money reality is the first step in identifying the underwater part of the iceberg (the 90 per cent).

- *Needs* is the most basic motivation. We need to look after our basic needs, such as food and shelter.
- Decision-making *drivers* are the way we place worth on an item or experience—in monetary, functional, social and psychological ways.
- *Values* are our personal concept of what's good, important, useful, desirable, constructive and so on. These are our deepest motivators.

Each person's journey is unique and our experiences shape our beliefs. Everyone has their own path. It has more to do with us than anything else, although it's influenced by our parents, our environment and life events.

Let's now look at each of the three motivators in more detail.

Back to basics: the needs hierarchy

Back in 1943 Abraham Maslow published a paper about people and motivation. It's pretty well known, but here's a quick reminder. Maslow initially identified five levels of human need and suggested that each level had to be (mostly) satisfied in order for us to move up a level. The hierarchy is drawn as a pyramid with our basic needs—being things like shelter and water—at the bottom, moving up through safety to belongingness, and so on. Over the years he refined his theory and introduced an additional three levels.

Transcendence
helping others (to self-actualise)

Self-actualisation
personal growth, fulfilment

Aesthetic needs
beauty, balance, form, etc.

Cognitive needs
knowledge, meaning, self-awareness

Esteem needs
achievement, status, responsibility, reputation

Belongingness and love needs
family, affection, relationships, workgroup, etc.

Safety needs
protection, security, order, law, limits, stability, etc.

Biological and physiological needs
basic life needs — air, food, drink, shelter, warmth, sex, sleep, etc.

Having a sense of Maslow's hierarchy and the way people prioritise things can give a sense of comfort to your spending. We need to be able to tick off the levels (in order). For example, in developed countries, most of the population can tick off level 1: access to clean water, food and so on. The second level is about safety. We want a secure home and to be able to go about our day in safety—and for the most part we can. When we've met these needs, we can move up to the next level of the pyramid, belongingness and love. However, we sometimes confuse *consumption* with our *needs*—for example, eating a meal at a fancy restaurant doesn't sit at the base level of Maslow's hierarchy!

If you're a Spender or a Slender, you may find that your motivation to move from the lower levels happens a little too quickly. Our needs are subjective. In a modern, developed country, the way we define the required basic level of food or our home as meeting our needs, for example, is personal and varies. You can spend a little, or a lot.

So your needs, and your perceptions of them, represent the first motivator of your spenditude underneath the water. We all know this, but we don't always have it front of mind.

What's driving your choices?

Every purchase we make (or choose not to make) is driven by the way we prioritise four key factors: *monetary, functional, psychological* and *social*. Spenders, Slenders and Defenders all prioritise these in different ways. The order in which you consider they apply pushes you towards or away from the purchase.

Let's explain that a bit more.

Spenders are most likely to place emphasis on social and psychological worth ('I want to look good'; 'Purchasing makes me happy'). Social and psychological influences drive their purchasing decisions.

Defenders prioritise functional and monetary worth ahead of social and psychological influences ('Is this a good financial choice?'; 'Will it bring me value over time?'; 'Is it the most functional option?'; 'Will it last?').

Slenders move between drivers. Each will take priority at different times and for different purchases. Sometimes Slenders feel that those social pressures are more important than monetary value and they'll spend more than they wanted to. At other times, Slenders will look to the functional importance well ahead of the social influences. So their ranking of drivers shifts and changes.

Think about a recent purchase you made, be it an item or an experience. How do you rank functional, social, monetary and psychological worth in relation to this item? Also consider where it fits on Maslow's hierarchy.

Take a shirt, for example. You can spend a little or a lot on it. Is it a basic need in Maslow's hierarchy? We all need clothing. Or does it represent achievement and status (esteem needs, level 4)? Do you prioritise the function of the shirt or the social value? If you're prioritising social needs and the related psychological needs, you're placing more emphasis on the feeling you have about the item than the price.

If you're a Spender, you're more likely to buy the expensive, branded shirt because the social and psychological drivers are higher on your list. Those 'likes' on social media, the thrill of the purchase, are important.

A Defender might buy the shirt, but with a key difference: they'll consider that the quality of the shirt provides them with more value over time. It's not about brand or social perception. Defenders buy within their financial ability. They place monetary cost and function above the other drivers.

The problem that Slenders have is that they shift the ranking of the drivers for each purchase. They haven't really confirmed in their mind the reason for the choice: do they think the shirt is the best choice functionally because they perceive it to be better quality (like a Defender does)? Or do they feel like they want the social recognition (like a Spender does)? Slenders shuffle between the two, on that treadmill, never firmly ranking the four drivers.

But wait, there's a deeper motivation way at the bottom of the iceberg ...

Deep motivators

Back to the shirt. Let's say you have a clear value relating to the environment, society, ethics or quality—this will influence your purchase decision, regardless of the cost.

In this case, your personal values, your deep motivators, will underpin the purchase decision.

It's these deep motivational influences and values that drive our behaviour. They're never about money. Money is an emotional topic that can be exaggerated in our minds to help solve our problems. People believe that if they had more money they may be able to move their life to where they want it to be.

Whether you're a Defender, a Slender or a Spender, your personal, unique purpose, deep values and motivators could be around family, learning, creativity, generosity, security, consistency, leadership, independence, acceptance, integrity, love ...

For the most part, people aren't often conscious of their values and motivators. They're also not really aware of how these deep motivators can limit their choices. It's in discovering the treasure that is your values—the themes in your life, the deep motivations that drive your decisions—that you can bring clarity. All of these will stem back to experiences in childhood and life.

Lisa's story

Lisa's mum got the sack when she told her boss she was pregnant, so when Lisa came into the world money was tight. Her parents were genuinely struggling to make ends meet. Her mum wasn't working and her dad was studying. Lisa's grandad stepped in to help out. Supporting family was central to his values, despite the fact that his own father hadn't offered him the same assistance.

When her grandad emigrated from Italy, he came with nothing. His farming background had shown him that land meant security and also status. Working hard, saving and buying land made sense to him and he passed this on to his son (Lisa's dad). He didn't have big aspirations, but he had obligations to help and to provide for his family. The most important thing you could do was to provide a roof for your family; then extra money was saved to buy land (always houses, never apartments).

When Lisa was about ten she asked her mum why they were poor. The girls at school seemed keen to point out that she didn't wear brands and she certainly wasn't wearing the expensive Reeboks that some of the kids had. Her mum clearly pointed out that they weren't poor; things had improved over the years, but they were sensible with money. But Lisa really wanted the Reeboks, and her uncle quickly became her favourite when he returned from a business trip with a pair for her.

Lisa worked during high school and university, but her income was disposable — CDs, movies, a stereo system (it was okay to be a Spender). Soon after university finished Lisa was working full time and engaged to be married. Her father impressed upon her that she needed to be saving for a home: 'That's what you do when you're getting married — you must have a roof over your head.' It was a steep learning curve. Moving from no financial obligations to saving hard and then paying a mortgage taught Lisa to quickly tighten her spending.

Lisa feels fortunate for the head start her dad gave her. Starting young helped her to get established before having kids and has softened the financial stress that came with her second child, who has special needs. Owning property, working hard to pay it off and being generous with family has been passed from Lisa's grandad to her father and to her. She is concerned about this obligation to her children, with property prices being so high.

While money wasn't formally discussed in her childhood, there was always a sense that you had to be careful about your choices. Lisa works hard and is aware of the ins and outs in her bank accounts. She had great grounding in managing her money as a young child. Despite wanting to keep up with her friends, her parents showed her that having a long-term focus was more important. As an adult, she isn't bothered about brands or labels, although some additional disposable income wouldn't go astray.

Lisa has values around family and security that have been passed down from her parents and grandparents. Despite some experiences wanting to keep up with peers, she is a Defender with a long-term focus. Lisa doesn't prioritise brands and keeps cost and function at the forefront of her mind. With a special-needs child, Lisa is very aware of having to ensure her family is financially secure and that their baseline needs are met.

According to James M. Kouzes and Barry Z. Posner, authors of *The Leadership Challenge*, individuals who are clear about their values have higher levels of commitment, pride and happiness in their work. However, determining your values isn't always the easiest of exercises. One way to attempt to get a sense of your values is to look at moments in your life and your responses to them.

- Can you think of a moment when you felt really satisfied with life? What was going on? What brought about those feelings?
- If you look back at the past month, or if someone was watching you for a month, what would they say was important to you?
- If your child was moving out of home, what would be the one thing you would want them to hang on to? What's the one piece of advice you would give them?
- What has made you happy? What has made you wise?
- How do you handle the tough days and moments? This is just as important to understanding your values as the moments of happiness.
- What do you absolutely know to be true about life, love, happiness … ?
- If you had to explain this time in your life at some point in the future—that is, your reasons for the decisions you're making now—could you do it?

When we're trying to make big decisions or assess our values, there's often a sense of looking inwards. What does your head say? What does your heart say? This can be very difficult. So try looking at your behaviours to see what you can identify.

Too often we equate self-worth with net worth. Having the good life seems to mean defining ourselves through the lens that others perceive us through, or looking around us and identifying our values based on our community, family or culture. Theodore Roosevelt purportedly said, 'Comparison is the thief of joy.' How true. Comparing yourself to others will steal your money and your happiness. Challenge your thoughts about money and look for opportunities to be grateful.

Loving your decisions comes with knowing who you are — your deep motivations. A sense of self-confidence comes with learning more about who you are and what motivates you. In identifying your values you'll be able to feel happier and see more opportunity. You're on your own path, and no-one else's. You can't be certain about what's going to happen next, but you can be grateful for who you are and what you have.

What life are you living and what life do you want to live? Not in the sense of owning or acquiring things, but in the sense of your deepest pleasure and joy. Still struggling to be clear on your values? Check out the exercise at the end of this chapter.

The outcome is focus

Defenders are focused. They're aware of their needs and they don't climb Maslow's ladder too quickly. They prioritise their drivers. They know the value of patience.

Hold on! There's so much to understand! The 90 per cent of the iceberg below the water is really complicated so we've summarised the motivators — needs, drivers and values — in the table overleaf as they apply to our three spenditude categories to help you work out where you fit.

	Needs *Maslow's Hierarchy of Needs*	**Drivers** *Social, monetary, psychological, functional*	**Values** *Personal, unique purpose; deep motivators*
Spenders	Are focused on their wants, and their needs may not be in order	Are short term Social and psychological drivers come first	Aren't very clear on these
	Spenders may be more focused on belonging and esteem (Maslow's levels 3 & 4) so these may take precedence	*FOMO* *Borrow* *Look successful* *Self-interest* *Instant gratification* *Passion*	*Appearance comes before security*
Slenders	May move up the hierarchy too quickly Haven't quite fulfilled the lower-level needs before jumping higher. Are focused on survival	Are affected by life stage and the order of drivers changes regularly	Are somewhat clear
	Home *Car* *Job* *Professional development* *Retire successfully*	*Borrow* *Invest* *Guilt* *Envy*	

Defenders	Relate to values Slower to progress through the levels; ensure that foundations are strong before moving higher. Basic needs underpin choices	Discipline and delayed gratification Monetary and functional drivers always come first	Are clear and focused Re-assess as life moves on
	Home unencumbered	*Invest in what they understand*	
	Own car	*Save*	
	Professional development	*Delay gratification*	
	Good lifestyle	*Understand tax, rewards, investments, compound interest*	
	Invest in their passion		
	Retire early	*Borrow to create appreciating assets*	
	Are savvy	*Avoid waste*	
	Educate kids about money	*Create legacy*	

A Spender named Anna (part 3)

As shown in chapter 4, community has become the driving force in Anna's life. Despite the rocky path that she faced when her parents split, Anna had seen the issues in her wider community and could contrast them to other towns, cities and experiences. Violence, teen mums and dads, and placing priority on the social aspect of spending was a cycle that she wanted to help break.

In a time of stress and change, she had a door-slamming moment. Anna became clear on her values.

Leadership. Perseverance. Community.

Anna went to university and her spending patterns changed through necessity. She learned to take control of her money and to maintain focus on her values.

Anna was appointed to a director's role in her community organisation when she was just 33 years old. She is dedicated to helping make financial and community decisions to improve outcomes for her people.

Anna has climbed the ladder from Spender to Defender.

In the next chapter we take you into the jungle where tigers are looming and awareness is key.

Be true to what's true to you:

I understand my deep motivators and values and I'll become true to them.

Under the water

There are many ways to understand and determine your values. One of the simplest ways is to look at a list of possible values—like the one below—and cross off the ones that you feel aren't important to you. This reduces the list quickly. Repeat the exercise of crossing out values for a second time and even a third. This becomes harder as the list becomes shorter.

Abundance	Consistency	Fun
Acceptance	Contribution	Future
Accountability	Courage	Generosity
Achievement	Creativity	Grace
Acknowledgement	Credibility	Growth
Advancement	Curiosity	Happiness
Adventure	Daring	Health
Advocacy	Decisiveness	Honesty
Aid	Dedication	Humility
Ambition	Dependability	Humour
Appreciation	Development	Inclusiveness
Attractiveness	Diligence	Independence
Autonomy	Discipline	Individuality
Balance	Diversity	Initiative
Being the best	Education	Innovation
Benevolence	Efficiency	Inspiration
Boldness	Empathy	Integrity
Brilliance	Encouragement	Intelligence
Calmness	Enjoyment	Intimacy
Caring	Enthusiasm	Intuition
Challenge	Environment	Joy
Charity	Ethics	Justice
Cheerfulness	Excellence	Kindness
Cleverness	Expressiveness	Knowledge
Communication	Fairness	Leadership
Community	Faith	Learning
Commitment	Family	Legacy
Compassion	Friendships	Love
Competence	Flexibility	Loyalty
Contribution	Freedom	Making a
Cooperation	Frugality	difference
Collaboration	Fulfilment	Meaning

Mindfulness
Motivation
Openness
Optimism
Originality
Passion
Peace
Perfection
Performance
Perseverance
Playfulness
Popularity
Power
Preparedness
Privacy
Proactiveness
Professionalism
Punctuality
Quality

Recognition
Relationships
Reliability
Resilience
Resourcefulness
Respect
Responsibility
Responsiveness
Risk-taking
Safety
Savviness
Security
Self-control
Selflessness
Serenity
Service
Simplicity
Spirituality
Stability

Success
Teamwork
Thankfulness
Thoughtfulness
Traditionalism
Trust
Truthfulness
Understanding
Uniqueness
Usefulness
Variety
Versatility
Vision
Warmth
Wellbeing
Wisdom
Work

Chapter 6

Where's the tiger?

Imagine being trapped in the jungle with one other person.

Nightfall is approaching and you can hear the roar of native animals. 'What was that?' you ask yourself, unsure that your companion is even awake to the potential hazards ahead.

Now imagine if your companion actually knows where the tiger that's lurking in the bushes is (and you don't).

Their awareness will almost certainly lead to more informed choices, putting them in a better position than you. Awareness gives them a significant advantage.

The point to the story is *awareness* is key. If you're aware of your spenditude, values and narrative, you're in a much better position to make better choices and changes.

Awareness = better decisions.

Awareness = reducing the risk of insanity.

Being aware of the tiger = improving your spenditude.

Albert Einstein is purported to have said that 'insanity is doing the same thing over and over and expecting a different result'.

Tight five

Moving into the third decade of the new millennium, the only constant will be more change as the digital revolution and political uncertainty continue on their rampant paths. The future is exciting for some and scary for many. In such unprecedented change, one thing's for sure: to be prepared we must ensure we have our financial house in order. Global research confirms that the majority of the population is stressed about money and it causes unwanted anxiety (Prudential Wellness Report, 2017). Most people feel they have no control over their financial future. What an awful thought...No. Control. Over. Your. Financial. Future.

What are the five key actions—the tight five—that will help you create awareness?

1. Make a little plan and pivot
2. Spend less than you earn
3. Our second Einstein quote
4. Warren says...
5. Mindfulness

1. Make a little plan and pivot

Create awareness by making a plan. Goal setting has long been known as a tool to increase our chances of achieving something. Research by Dr Gail Matthews of the Dominican

University of California suggests that you increase your odds by 42 per cent by writing down your goals. Sharing your goals with a friend increases that percentage even further.

When you write things down you store the information somewhere external to create a visual cue. If you see the cue regularly, you're more likely to remember it. But the interesting part of writing things down is the way it's stored in your brain. When you write things down it improves the encoding process in your brain to help you remember what you wrote. These two combined give you a greater chance of success.

When you make a plan, try starting with small changes, breaking down goals into smaller parts (a 'little' plan). When we set big goals — such as 'pay off the mortgage' — without smaller milestones along the way and without the opportunity to celebrate small wins, we're more likely to fail. Work with your human emotions and psychology and build momentum. We all need positive feedback or reinforcement to succeed and we're more interested in continuing something if we see more immediate results.

Remember, if you set yourself a goal and you fall off the wagon (on day 2, week 2, month 2 or beyond) you're the one who controls the response. Don't quit because of one mistake.

Say you had a goal to reduce your spending on takeaway food, or taxis, or to reduce your debt — what rules are you setting? Is it okay to eat out or take a cab once a week or once a month? Have you placed a specific value and a date on the debt? What if your taxi was really cheap: are you going to convince yourself that it doesn't 'count'? If you're trying to pay a particular amount of money off your debt and you don't meet your goal, do you give up? Do you re-frame the goal?

It's great to have a goal to save money on food or cabs or to pay off debt. But what's the end game you're pushing towards? Make a plan. Are the savings you're making helping to build your emergency fund? Will the money ensure you don't put that next holiday on credit? Is it to free up some income to put towards your 'Weekend' (see chapter 3), or is it to simplify your life with less stuff?

Set yourself a realistic challenge. Re-visit. Consider. Write it down! Take deliberate action. Your first 'little plan' can be just that — little. Remember: momentum.

What can you do to increase your chances of making the plan stick? With all the best intentions, how many times have you started a diet, commenced an exercise regime or wanted to give up something that you know is no good for you, and not succeeded in the longer term? Perhaps you set your goal on New Year's Day and stuck to it throughout January and then life took over and you yielded to old habits.

How are you motivating yourself to reach the goal? With fear or rewards? If you were explaining to someone else why this goal is important, what would you say? You need a sense of *why* you've set the goal (and it shouldn't be 'because I must do this').

Writing it down is great, but add a second mini action plan: how are you going to make the change? What's your day-to-day plan? What's influencing your responses and trying to drag your spenditude back? Don't stick with old familiar habits — find your strengths. For example, if you love reading, use this as an alternative activity to keep you away from another habit you're trying to change (and borrow the books, don't buy them).

Don't let your plan revolve around 'earning more' as your primary focus. Earning more doesn't cure your spenditude. It's easier to cut costs than it is to increase your income. Keeping up with the Joneses or living the same life as though something will magically change doesn't work. Make a plan.

Pivot for success

You've made that plan and built into it some smaller milestones. But life has a way of taking us off track.

If you find yourself straying, pivot and get back on track. If you find your path is changing, pivot again and revise your plan. As you work towards the goal, continue to pivot at each step. Keep the goal realistic and if life shifts the goal posts or that door slams in your face, don't drop the ball.

So how do you stay on track?

- *Celebrate small wins.* If you don't incentivise yourself you're more likely to fail. Be reasonable.
- *Research.* You can't change a lifetime habit without learning something new: something that spurs you to action, something that changes the way you see your habit, something that makes you want to change.
- *Practise and train.* Habit change only comes with repetition. Even the best athletes keep up their training.
- *Review.* Review your plan, continue to pivot and enhance your skills. No matter your level of knowledge and no matter how big your goal, maintaining the sense that you can find a new way of doing things can help you achieve the goal.

Once you're in the black, you should never go back (to red)

This reminds us of the story (in chapter 1) of the people in the restaurant talking about money. Andrew, when talking to his partner Lucy, got great delight out of showing her an Excel spreadsheet that demonstrated how to manage money and stay in the black. 'She was amazed and since then we've had a combined money narrative and plan, which is to stay in the black.'

What was it about this Excel spreadsheet that changed her spenditude?

The default position for Defenders is to stay in the black. They don't want to be in debt unless it's for necessary assets, such as a home, but even then they're keen to eliminate the mortgage as quickly as possible (see our second Einstein quote, on page 116).

For Slenders, this is a constant challenge and struggle. How do I manage my finances so I'm going forwards and not backwards? Staying in the black is a goal but not always a reality.

Spenders would simply switch off if you showed them an Excel spreadsheet, so we don't recommend doing that just now.

So, Slenders need to look at basic habit changes to move from red to black (negative to positive) on a constant basis. These habits are fundamental and in the past were a pain to complete. For most it was about tracking your money on a piece of paper or spreadsheet manually. And they gave up within two months (or sooner). Now we have technology that can track your spending, provide alerts when you overspend and, more importantly, provide you with simple awareness of where the money is being spent. No more spreadsheets, no more notebooks. It's automated and it's usually free with the service you receive from your bank. If not, there are plenty of apps out there to help you.

We're more likely to forgo small purchases in favour of large savings goals when we have smaller targets. Reframe your shift into black with smaller sub-goals and they'll feel more attainable, which will help you accumulate more savings over the longer term.

Which brings us to our second key action…

2. Spend less than you earn

This is the oxygen that drives wealth creation (or wealth deflation).

The advice you're most likely to receive when asking a Defender about the key to financial success is 'to spend less than you earn'. It seems like a simple idea, but as we increasingly move away from cash as a society, we have less 'pain of paying'. This, combined with easy access to credit (Afterpay, anyone?) has meant that spending less than you earn isn't as simple as it once was. How can we change our habits to ensure we spend less than we earn?

Keep reading. We promise not to tell you to write some kind of restrictive budget.

Track it

Think about your spenditude as having two key categories— controllable (wants) and inevitable (needs)—with a sub-category within 'discretionary' for passion spending. It's okay to spend money on things you have a passion for, such as hobbies; it's okay to have a 'passion budget'—in fact, it's important. One of the reasons people fail to spend less than they earn is simply because they have no awareness of how much is in each of the categories.

We have mental categories of money and we label money in our minds both before and after we spend it. Consider the labels. Which category is it coming out of and how much is in that category right now? In order to know, you need to have *awareness* of how much of your income should be allocated to each category. Inevitable items are the bills, the rent, the things you have less control over. The controllable category has two parts: hobbies/passions (the sub-category we mentioned above) and other controllable spending (e.g. food and beverage, transport and day-to-day bills). This is where the waste lives. Identify where you're wasting money to help yourself move along the spenditude scale.

If you're a Spender or a Slender, leave the inevitable items and the hobbies/passions alone. Focus on your other controllable spending. Defenders, take this chance to re-assess your spending.

There's a long list of apps, wearables and systems that will help you to identify the waste. Start with your bank. Most banks have some kind of tracking tool, and most of them are quite good. At this stage you're trying to increase awareness. Technology has changed the game and there's no excuse not to prioritise your awareness.

If you're unaware of what's happening, you're exposed to the risk of spending more than you earn—of being slammed by a door—and you'll make poor financial decisions. These apps allow you to become aware, re-set your narrative and then track your success. It's never been easier to change the most fundamental habit: being aware of your finances and staying in the black.

The other key way to spend less than you earn is to...

Value it

Do you feel like you might suffocate if you buy one more thing? Are you triggered by emotions to spend? Buying something from the comfort of your lounge chair means putting less away for the bigger purchases/goals. We need to have a healthy respect for money in all its forms: actual money, plastic cards, online transactions, in-app purchases, phone payments, wearables...

For the most part, we make some kind of contribution of time/skill/effort in order to earn money, right? Consider how you can place real value on that purchase. We all have mental comparisons that help us see value. Providing a comparison can help put cost into perspective, for example:

- How many hours' work does the expense equate to?
- How much money per day/week/month would I need to save to pay for this?
- How many months' rent does it equate to?
- What am I missing out on if I purchase this?
- Is there a cheaper alternative?
- In what time frame will it feel like wasted money?
- What problem does it solve?
- Is my purchase based on genuine need or cultural/social pressure?
- Will it last? (quality, new technology, use-by date)
- Does this fuel my life? (emotion, mind, body, contentment)

Finding greater intention in your consumer habits will support financial outcomes and will help you spend less than you earn.

We see this a lot at Christmas time: kids writing Santa lists and asking for new things, and adults getting lost in what to buy everyone. But we also see how quickly the new toy is pushed aside (kids and adults alike). Are the best gifts actually experiences that create memories that you can remember and discuss? Making choices about how you spend your money includes an opportunity to be satisfied with what you have; to choose enjoyment and giving; and to have the strength to say no.

Back to a famous great mind…

3. Our second Einstein quote

Another fundamental from Einstein is 'Compound interest is the eighth wonder of the world. He who understands it, earns it...he who doesn't...pays it'.

We learn about compound interest at school, but do you really comprehend how big a part compound interest plays in our money and wealth creation?

Simply put, compound interest is when you earn interest on your interest. Say you deposit $100 in a bank account and earn $5 in interest at the end of the year, and you leave the full amount in your account. At the end of the second year you earn interest on the new balance of $105. There are loads of compound interest calculators online that can help you see how this can apply to your circumstances (moneysmart.gov.au is a great place to start).

Consider a $10 weekly deposit into a bank account ($520 per year) and no withdrawals. After 10 years you've deposited $5200 but have earned $1181 in interest (at 4 per cent p.a.). At the five-year mark you've earned only $273 in interest, notice how the upside as time passes is significant. (We've simplified the numbers and not taken into account changes in interest rates, tax on earnings and other variables.)

For the most part people understand this. For example, money placed into a retirement fund earlier in your career has bigger earning potential over time.

But it's the second part of Einstein's quote that's less obvious.

Paying interest on debt, be it credit cards or your home loan, is essentially paying compound interest. The earlier you make extra repayments the bigger the impact—that is, the less interest you'll pay. In the same way that the interest earned on a savings account will have an upswing, payments made at the beginning of your home loan will make a bigger difference to the overall cost of the loan.

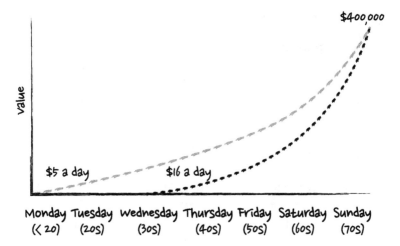

And now to another great mind…

4. Warren says…

Warren Buffett might just be the most successful investor of our time. He has several rules of investing.

His number one rule is 'Never lose money'.

Rule number two is 'Don't forget rule no. 1'.

He then advises us not to be frivolous, not to gamble and not to go into an investment with a cavalier attitude that it's okay to lose (are you listening, Spenders?).

Finally, he confirms that you must invest in something you understand. Do your research. Be informed.

There are a million good books on how to invest, and this is not one of them. Perhaps go Barefoot next?

Debt and saving

Are they opposite sides of the same coin?

Some people are good at paying down debt and others are good at saving. It's interesting because both require discipline and some sort of plan.

Are you a saver or a debt payer? Can you be both?

Numerous studies have revealed that people who are savers tend to preserve their savings for their intended use, even while holding debt. Even when an emergency strikes. We seem to focus on one or the other. Banking products tend to support this, with credit cards and savings accounts not always closely aligned.

Holding cash—just enough for your emergency fund—is important. Beyond that, cash savings are not an investment. Over time, with inflation, cash depreciates in value—other investments perform much better than cash does. So, having too much cash sitting around could be a lost opportunity.

So read some more, learn some more and invest in what you understand (just like Warren says).

Good debt and bad debt

Identify your debt and have a plan.

Bad debt is borrowing for assets that lose value immediately. Cars, holidays and lifestyle come to mind as examples. The only time a Defender would borrow money for a depreciating asset would be if the loan was interest and fee free for a short period of time. An example is the credit card: if you pay your bill every month you avoid paying any interest. There are fees for these types of cards, but the point is that you can borrow someone else's money and pay no interest if you are organised. On top of that you can gain frequent flyer points to fund your next holiday. The big trap is not being organised to pay down the full amount on the due date. This is the Spender's trap and the Defender's strategy—it's a real Defender special. It only works if you're aware.

One strategy for repaying debt is to start with the bill with the highest interest rate and pay that down as soon as possible. You then go to the one with the next highest interest rate and pay that down. Avoid high interest rates. They're high for a reason. Supply and demand. You want the money for stuff that you probably don't need and they lend it to you at a high rate. This repayment method is generally called a 'debt avalanche' or 'stacking'.

The other strategy is to pay down the smallest debt first and to keep moving along the list from smallest to biggest. This works to build momentum. Look up 'Dave Ramsey Snowball' to find out more about this method. The debt snowball works to human psychology because you gain momentum more quickly. If you have a lot of debts, this is a worthwhile strategy. The choice to pay down small ones helps give you feedback that you can move forward and get rid of your debt.

Good debt is borrowing funds to create assets. Defenders borrow money to purchase shares or investment properties. These are generally appreciating assets, but not always. It's a sophisticated way of using debt and should be closely monitored and advised. There are traps such as the asset going down in value at the same time as interest rates rise. This double whammy generates much pain.

Necessary debt is borrowing money to buy a house. Ever more people under the age of 'Thursday' are deciding to avoid this concept—they're the so-called Generation Rent. When borrowing large amounts over a long time (as for a mortgage) it's best to remember Einstein's eighth wonder: compound interest. It works in reverse (see the previous section). The longer the term, the more interest you pay.

So debt is a friend and an enemy. Perhaps even a frenemy. Understanding it and using it correctly is the best path to follow.

Check out this simple concept—we call it the 'Defender's money central'—that illustrates how Defenders think. They're constantly and automatically aware of where their money is coming from and going to, and when. This is a key component of awareness.

The Defender's money central

The key to the Defender's money central is its simplicity and focus.

Money IN is quite simple. Just consider what sort of account your income should be landing in. There may be benefits in offsetting your mortgage, for instance. Investments could be shares, property or cash.

Money OUT is where the magic can start.

Controllable expenses other than those related to hobbies/passion is where Defenders make savings. They use their value lens and also track their spending to ensure this expense category doesn't get out of hand.

Inevitable is more difficult to reduce. However, Defenders are all over these as well. They ensure they pay minimum tax, have the kids' expenses and education covered, and they only have debt that creates an asset or is interest free. They also shop around for the best deals on utilities and insurance.

Passion is a different thing. Having funds available to enjoy what you love is critical. For many, having funds aside for experiences rather than assets is a priority. For others, it's making sure there's enough around for the annual holiday. If you can't do what you love doing, what's the point?

For the big passion items, you must set a goal—remember that you're more likely to achieve smaller goals (see section 1 of this chapter).

That leads us to our fifth and final key awareness action...

5. Mindfulness

Addicted to spending? ('I need some retail therapy.') Hey, Big Spenders, this one's for you.

Chelsea Pottenger, an Australian mindfulness expert, notes 'Overspending is omnipresent' (adjective: widespread or constantly encountered). Going a step further, Lisa Messenger, author of *Money and Mindfulness*, states, 'Money mindsets and attitudes can affect our chances of succeeding.'

Does being happy and peaceful have a link to our spenditude? Yes. The investment in getting your sleep right and then changing your narrative through mindfulness or meditation may well take away the urge for Spenders to need retail therapy hits.

Addiction is real. Research is exploring the link between happiness and addiction. It was once thought that addiction was genetic or related to a chemical hook. However, studies with rats (it's always those poor old rats) in the 1970s by Bruce Alexander, a professor of Psychology in Vancouver, demonstrated a link between happiness and addiction.

Rats were in a cage and had two sources of liquid: water, and heroin or cocaine in water.

The first experiment was in a hostile and uncomfortable environment. The rats were stressed out and subsequently preferred the heroin/cocaine water. The second was in a peaceful environment where there was no stress and the rats' preference was the plain water.

Okay, it's not quite that simple for us. The rats' happy little playground is not the same as the complexity of our modern lives. But the experiment does get us thinking about addiction and spending.

Does our spenditude have a link to addiction? The dopamine in our brain is released in anticipation of happiness. So if you think you're addicted to shopping, online shopping is worse because the anticipation of receiving something in the mail lasts longer than in a store and as you become used to the dopamine 'hit' you look for more. Trying to ride the wave of anticipation without clicking that 'buy now' button may actually help you reduce your addiction.

Houston... I might have a problem

Changing behaviour and curing addictions is an industry. Stop smoking, stop drinking, stop gambling…Behaviour change programs are generally offered to those who have come to the realisation that they have a problem. The most famous one is the 12-step program originally developed for Alcoholics Anonymous, but now adapted for most forms of addiction. Step 1 is the key to the program: be aware and admit that this behaviour is affecting your life. If you don't pass step 1, you can't do the other 11 steps—because if you don't admit you have a problem, you won't change. The same goes for your spenditude.

Mindfulness = awareness.

What is mindfulness?

Mindfulness is a widely overused term delivered in many different forums, apps, books and podcasts. If we can focus on the use of mindfulness to assist us to prepare for money habit change, then we need to dig a bit deeper into what we're trying to solve.

As we've seen, money habits are deeply rooted and our money narrative and values may not match our desired behaviour. So with all this noise going on we face an uphill battle to focus. This is where mindfulness can help.

Let's borrow a definition from the wonderful Australian charity SANE Australia:

> Mindfulness is a mental and physical technique you can use to focus your awareness on the present moment. Mindfulness practice is simple, powerful, takes just a few minutes and can be done almost anywhere, so it is a great addition to your mental health self-care.

SANE Australia supports the mental health of Australians affected by complex mental illness. Mindfulness is a key strategy. It works.

So if mindfulness can assist someone severely affected by mental health to focus on the present moment, it can assist Spenders (and others) to become more aware of their spending.

We asked Australian mindfulness expert Chelsea Pottenger...

How would you explain mindfulness?

> Mindfulness is the practice of bringing your attention to the present. It is about reconnecting with positive aspects in your life, like your health, family and friendships.

> Practising gratitude for what you have is a very simple way to hardwire your brain for more gratefulness, kindness and happiness.

Can mindfulness help us manage our money?

> Mindfulness can help us see why we are really spending and deal with it appropriately. It can help us to make better decisions by allowing us to live in the moment. When you are thinking about spending, mindfulness allows you to notice where your mind goes.

> Overspending is omnipresent. Thousands of people have been increasing their spend as a way to cope and escape from daily pressures and decrease stress. 'If only I had a...I would achieve success' are common reactions to the social media phenomena.

How does mindfulness work?

When we are anxious, the body responds by speeding up and we take in more oxygen and breathe out more carbon dioxide than normal. However, because the body isn't working any harder, this leads to a temporary change in the pH of the blood. The good news is that this pattern can be changed. Just as our feelings influence how we breathe, how we breathe can influence and affect our feelings.

How we breathe dictates every internal process in your brain and body.

Meditation is actually proven to shrink the amygdala in our brains. This is where our stress lives. This allows you to stay calmer when you experience those stress triggers. In fact, meditation has positive impacts on all the parts of our brain. Mindfulness practice is just like a little mini meditation to bring you back to the present and help you.

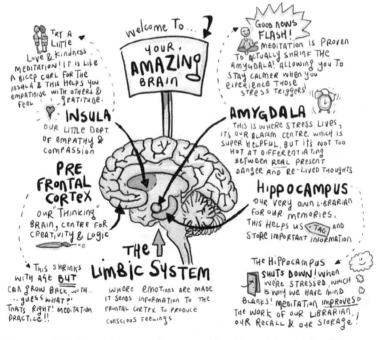

Source: EQ Consulting co (eqconsultingco.com) and Catfish-Creative (catfishcreative.com.au)

Chelsea's comments echo all the research around overspending. Spenders tend to use 'retail therapy' as just that—therapy.

Our mind, our self

It's our mind's job to generate thoughts, categorise them, analyse them and tell a 'story'. Remember your money narrative from chapter 4 about purchasing 'things' to distract yourself from the present or from that voice in your head? Mindfulness is a tool that can help change that habit. It's easy to get caught in the story, worry, comparison or guilt.

Consider your mindset now, and a year ago. Did you see yourself as wanting more—for example, a new item that would bring you happiness? Did that purchase bring you long-lasting joy? Consistently buying material things is not the answer—and mindfulness can help give us the pause we need to make different choices.

As well as being a tool that we can use to find that pause, mindfulness is also a method of initiating self-reflection and bringing increased self-awareness. Developing this self-awareness is essential in achieving transformation of habits, behaviours and experiences. It can bring new awareness to your 'story'. If you don't acknowledge that story, it will shape how you behave, what you see and how you feel—and that has a self-fulfilling loop. So Spenders who believe they're 'bad with money' can use mindfulness to take the time to consider their thoughts and their story. If you fail to take into account this background and noise in your mind, the behaviour is self-fulfilling. Spenders will then continue to be 'bad with money'.

Dr Mark Ryan (from chapter 2) suggested that these conceptualisations constitute our sense of self and are largely in the service of social survival and functioning. We default to an unquestioning belief in what our thoughts tell us and we can get 'trapped' in that story. Mindfulness can help us be calm and begin to 'see' this story. Further meditation and contemplation can enable us to identify and 'drop' these thoughts.

Alternatively, cognitive behavioural therapy (CBT) approaches can be used. These involve developing helpful and adaptive thoughts so you become more flexible and responsive, rather than reactive and habitual. In other words, they enable you to become more considered and reflective, and to behave more in terms of what's actually happening (as opposed to what you think/believe is happening). In relation to your values, this can assist in keeping you more on track with respect to your goals and therefore more committed to reaching them.

Too often, what our minds present us with is 'construction noise on a busy road' (that is, 'self, meaning, other and world'). Once we identify these kinds of thoughts it's important to ignore them. It can also be helpful to note that thoughts are always about something/someone and are self-referential—that is, self-serving.

Of course, you can't get a handle on how your brain makes up your mind for you if you don't get enough sleep. Too little sleep means you have a diminished chance of changing and you'll likely continue pursuing the same old spending and saving habits. The market economy thrives on such mindlessness. We're busy opening up thoughts and we need to 'train our brains not to listen'—that is, to ignore the busy thoughts.

Back in the jungle

Imagine you're back in the jungle. You now know the location of the tiger. Your only decision now is 'Do I act now or wait?'

Don't wait … act now.

Quick decisions are critical when walking through a jungle populated by tigers. If you have a gun in the jungle you probably don't want to hurt any animals; however, you do want to use it for effect.

There's no time to procrastinate in the jungle. The same goes for habit-changing money rituals. You can pick up your rifle and:

- Ready, Aim, Aim, Aim, Aim, Aim, Aim (never making the choice to fire)
- Ready, Fire, Aim (I just jumped right in)
- Ready, Aim, Fire (the calm person wins).

The trick to changing your spenditude is to start.

So, once you've finished reading this book, come back to this chapter to get yourself started so you're ready to aim and then fire.

And now for *the most critical first step in the history of first steps*: create this New Reality and you're on your way.

Your goal only needs to be one month to begin with. Remember: baby steps.

In month 2, see if you can stay in the black and save 10 per cent of your income. Put it into your 'tomorrow' account. (Any old bank account just to keep it away from you—even under the bed if you like. Just make sure it doesn't get spent.)

Now you've gone two months in the black and you've saved 10 per cent of your income. That wasn't so hard, was it? Try giving it another go next month.

By month 3 you'll have reached your New Reality. You've tried black and you're not going back! You can feel a movement in your spenditude and it feels good!

In chapter 7 we move from mindfulness and understanding your own mind, to being tricked into spending. We dive into what psychologists know about how you spend your money that you might not.

Beware of the tiger:

I'll try to keep in the black and be aware of my finances.

Money-saving tips

There are hundreds of ways to save money or spend less. Google 'money saving tips' to find ideas. Here are our top 20 spenditude tips that you can implement right now. Remember that small changes can help you shift your spenditude.

1. $$$ for mindfulness

Use mindfulness to help reduce your purchases, then take a percentage of the value of what you wanted to buy and transfer it to your savings account. For example, you didn't buy a shirt that was $50, so 10 per cent of the value (or $5) goes towards your savings. When you transfer it, label the transaction record with what you didn't purchase.

2. Do a fast

Pick something that you feel you spend too much on and do a fast for a day, a week or a month. For example, reduce your grocery bill by not doing any grocery shopping for a month and use what's in the pantry and freezer. Of course, top up the fresh stuff and essentials. Or simply have Tight Tuesdays, where you try not to buy anything.

3. Financial journalling

Journalling can help you celebrate because you can see the achievements you've made. Do it daily or weekly, but no less often, to keep it top of mind. Write down a couple of small goals and commit to them. Write down the money thoughts you have each day. Writing down all the money that comes in brings awareness to it, to help you stop overspending. Writing down your financial anxieties helps address them. There are many ways to keep track of your spending and thoughts about spending.

4. Be specific

Create a plan and set specific goals—being intentional is key (what, when, and where), For example, 'I will save $150 by 1 April to have a nice birthday dinner out so I won't have to put it on credit'; or 'I'll pay off $400 of my credit card when I get paid on Wednesday. Go as big as you want; set smaller challenges along the way and celebrate them.

5. Front of mind

Change the password on your computer to reflect your goal. Put a picture of your plan or goal on your phone so you see it every day. Use that picture space in your wallet for your goal in picture or word form. Write it on a piece of paper and use it as your bookmark. Bringing your desires to the front of your mind helps you make choices every day.

6. Gamify

Make it a bit more fun and challenge yourself. Draw a chart and colour it in as you work towards your goal.

Make a bingo grid and each day/week tick off some of the values by putting your change into a money box.

Make a list of financial goals and give them points. When you get a certain number of points, reward yourself.

$0.50	$0.50	$0.50	$0.50
$0.50	$1.00	$1.00	$2.00
$0.50	$1.00	$2.00	$5.00
$1.00	$2.00	$5.00	$5.00
$2.00	$5.00	$5.00	$10.00

100%
80%
60%
40%
20%

90%
70%
50%
30%
10%

OUR GOAL

Thank you!

7. Use cash

It increases what's referred to as 'the pain of paying'. Also, delete your credit card details from your computer, making it harder to buy online.

8. The B word

A budget is important. Think of it as a money tracker: do it just to see where the spend is. This will be more helpful than trying to guess. Log in to your bank and see what they have to offer. It's the simplest and quickest way. Placing significant restrictions will only help you to fail. Knowing how much you spend now brings awareness.

9. Presence not presents

If you read about kids and behaviour you'll find an underlying theme: they want your presence more than anything else. Try not to buy things for them to replace your presence. This goes for relationships too.

10. Don't multitask

Focus on what you're spending. Watching television and shopping online is not a good combo.

11. What would a Defender do?

Look for extras that can help you change habits: sell that brand-new dress that still has the tags and you never wore (even if you get less $$ for it—at least the money is coming back to you). Take your bottles to the recycling machine to collect the cash. Take your old video games with you when buying a new one and trade them in. Cook in bulk; turn off the lights; wear a jumper instead of turning on the heater. Consciously ask yourself what a Defender would do in the situation.

12. Cheerleaders

Tell your plan to someone close to you. They will help hold you accountable. Saying it out loud and committing to it is proven to help. Want to be more anonymous? Check out stickk.com. This website helps you set a goal and stick to it by getting cheerleaders for you as well as having some other strategies to assist.

13. Cancel, cancel, cancel

Do you use the subscriptions, gym membership or tech that you're paying for? Be real.

14. Hit the library

There are so many free courses, services and opportunities available at libraries, not to mention *free* books. Also, it takes your time away from places where you can spend money.

15. Work with benefits

This can be worth hundreds if not thousands. Defenders know that companies have programs and extras that you can tap into at work. Get on the intranet, ask HR, ask colleagues: is there a discount on your health fund, a tax deduction, a study program, an opportunity that you can access to save you money and increase your skills?

16. Sleep better

Read chapter 2.

17. *Round it off*

Round off your bank balance each week. For example, if your bank account has a balance of $563.50, transfer $13.50 to your debt, savings account or retirement fund and round it down to $550. There are also apps that will round off your spending. For example, Raiz invests your round-ups in the share market. ING's Everyday Round Up account will also do this for you and the money can help you pay off your home loan.

18. *Gratitude*

Re-read the section in this chapter on mindfulness. Most of us live well. Yet, we don't appreciate it. Remove the resentfulness, greed or entitled attitude. Be grateful.

19. *Start with something*

Start by logging into your retirement account.

Start by knowing your hourly wage.

Start by selling one item.

Start by...

What can you accomplish today in order to begin? Focus. Make it a priority.

20. *Don't overstock*

If you think of money as inventory in your warehouse, you would always carry enough stock to meet the needs of your business. But you would try not to overstock. The only way you can know whether you're carrying the right amount, too much or too little, is to track it and be aware. *Awareness* is the ultimate key.

Chapter 7

This intelligence isn't artificial

Why can't you bend a coin in half? Because change is hard.

Human behaviour is a curious thing to observe. Just when you think you get it, it surprises you. However, one thing that's consistent is that people rarely like to change anything unless there's some form of benefit. Change for change's sake just doesn't work.

When we try to exercise willpower there's a lot working against us, from marketers to social cues and even the dopamine in your brain. Having a little understanding of the trips and traps can help you enhance your spenditude.

Mind games or marketing magic?

There are plenty of marketing tricks out there; some are more obvious than others.

'Would you like fries with that?'

'Free trial period'

'Free shipping when you spend $100'

'Only $2 a day'

We know that supermarkets put the milk in the back corner so we have to walk down aisles and past many other items to get to it. We know that the cheap bits and pieces near the checkout are there to make us add extra items to our shopping bag. We're cynical of product placement in television shows. Items at eye level, markdowns and floor plans all influence our spending.

Marketers know more about our behaviour than we do! Extending our knowledge a little further can help us make better choices and better decisions with our money.

Most people know that grocery shopping when you're hungry leads to a bigger bill at the checkout. We tend to have less ability to control our impulses when we're distracted, tired, 'hangry' or stressed. Is controlling your willpower something you have difficulty with? While good eating, exercise and sleep (see chapter 2) are helpful in building your willpower muscle (the prefrontal cortex), what else should you know about willpower, marketing and our brains in order to make better choices?

Anchoring

Consider walking into a furniture store to find that the first item on display is one of the store's more expensive pieces. As you continue to walk around you've anchored that price point in your mind. So if the first item you saw was $3000, the other items in the shop that are less than $3000 are now cheaper in comparison.

Or consider a new piece of technology. The first release always comes with a big price tag. There are people willing to pay it. As time passes, the price comes down, but you're still anchored to the original price. So you weren't willing to hand over $1200 for a new phone and you possibly didn't want to spend $800 either, but in the context of the anchor point, $800 might seem reasonable.

Both of these examples relate to higher price points and not things we buy every day, but anchoring is something that can happen with any size purchase. It can also work the other way, where the anchor point is low, which makes spending more seem like a good idea.

The second-cheapest bottle of wine in restaurants is the one that's sold most often—people don't want to look cheap so they order the second one on the list. Many restaurants know this and the second-cheapest bottle is the one they make the most money on. It's got the biggest market share in terms of restaurant sales, so it's probably the cheapest wine they buy and has the biggest mark-up too.

BOGO strategies

Buy one, get one (BOGO) strategies are common in many stores, from supermarkets to clothing. When the first shirt costs $40, a second one for only $20 seems cheap as your anchor was $40. But these strategies are there to get you to spend more. 'Meal deals' at fast-food restaurants bundle goods. If you're planning to purchase the added fries and drinks, then the deal can be better value (but not always); however, in bundling the goods the stores are increasing your spend by reducing your decision-making effort and increasing convenience, which you may value over the time it takes to choose.

Bringing awareness to these strategies can help you decline them. Framing the choice as a loss can also help you resist. BOGO brings on a feeling that you gained something for a cheaper price — it's that excitement and anticipation of your 'prize'. It's the dopamine in your brain that makes you pursue pleasure. Dopamine is actually released in anticipation of the reward, so avoiding the shops and sticking with online shopping doesn't help either. The anticipation of receiving your package lasts longer and some research suggests that online shopping actually brings a higher level of excitement than in-store shopping.

Can you flick that switch in your brain to try and bring down the dopamine hit: will my future self be happier/better for having this extra item?

Getting your brain to produce that dopamine effect for other things (that cost less money) can be achieved with a little practice. What else brings with it a sense of anticipation? The next chapter of a book, the next episode of a show, chatting with a friend on the phone? Beware of the dopamine effect when shopping.

The Goldilocks effect

Remember Goldilocks? She wanted to eat the porridge that was not too hot or cold, but just right.

What if she had only had two choices? Hot, or cold?

We make choices in the context of what's around. We compare. We look for the Goldilocks option and often default to the middle alternative — the medium-sized coffee, the mid-range one. Organisations know this and offer three options in the knowledge that many people will choose the middle one in anything from food and drink sizes to health insurance options or technology upgrades.

We also look to recommendations and default options. In essence, we're looking for information that helps us make choices. We're looking for ease. What's the standard option? What are other people doing? Organisations are able to use this knowledge to nudge people in a particular direction.

What if Goldilocks had had more than three choices: big, small, salty, sweet, hot, cold, green bowl, white bowl...? How would this have influenced her choice?

Well, maybe she would have just walked away. When the choice feels too hard to make, we often just defer it. We can't decide. It seems difficult so we don't make a decision or a purchase.

The other way we may behave is to look for another option where the choices are easier or there's something to help us choose. What if the porridge was divided into categories to help you follow a path: big or small, then salty or sweet, then hot or cold, then green or white. Each choice is easier as it compares only two options. 'I'll have the small, sweet, hot one in green please.' If another brand makes the choice easier, you might just go with that.

When the choice is complicated we look to recommendations, social norms and what other people are doing. What's the default option? How can we minimise our chance of regretting our decision? If the default option is that we're all opted in, then participation will be higher.

Say an organisation had a standard process for new employees that everyone paid $10 a month into a charity fund. You can choose to opt out, but you understand that this is what most people do. The standard has been set (the default position). The process to stop the payments is clear, but it requires a couple of steps. Most people will continue to donate. However, if the opposite is true—if there are steps and procedures for a person to follow that allow them to donate to the charity, and additionally there's no apparent 'normal' way—then fewer people will work through the steps to start donating. What's the right thing for the company to do?

Why does Goldilocks matter?

We're irrational decision makers. By making choices and decisions in the context of what's around, what's easy, default or what others are doing, we don't always get it right.

We're essentially looking for the easy option, the mid range, the 'follow the herd' option. Any barriers will prevent action and if there's too much information, we just don't make a choice. We compare, we look for clues and we try to minimise regret. Finally, we care what other people are doing and what they think. If you think your social network is influencing your decisions, it may be worth considering who in your circle really displays the behaviours and motivators that you want in your life. Making decisions in the context of what's around also applies in terms of what you see as 'normal'.

Me of the future

According to the National Center for Biotechnology Information in the United States, people are much more likely to put money away in a savings account when they're shown an aged photo of themselves. It's called future self-continuity. The level of distance you have from your future self affects your choices.

In the context of health, we know we should eat right, exercise and not smoke, but we essentially care less for our future selves—we treat our future selves as though they're a friend, not us. Our level of connection to long-term outcomes is small.

The notion of future self presents many challenges to the imagination. The research shows that when we consider our future self, pain seems less vivid and we suffer 'empathy gaps'.

That is, we misunderstand how we'll feel in the future about decisions made in the present. The degree to which you're able to feel connected to your future self has a direct impact on your health, money and relationships. Estrangement from your future self makes saving for retirement feel like you're giving your money to a future stranger, which makes you less likely to invest in your weekend. Connection to their future self helps people appreciate that they're the recipient and consequently affects their decision making. They see themselves as a person they can help, and they want to.

Trouble is, it's hard to get your hands on an image of your future self!

Are you waiting for 'future you' to do something? News flash. There's no miraculous future version of yourself that has the focus, energy and drive to jump in there. Stop making a choice to WTF (Wait Til Friday). Taking no action is a choice in itself and it's not giving respect to the you of the future.

Another interesting thought is the concept of our 'death clock'. When do we think we'll die? It's a subconscious clock for many of us. We base this on scattered facts and perhaps our fatalist tendencies.

Forget about the death clock

Eve always thought her dad would outlast her mum. Her dad's family lived long. Some into their next Wednesday (100). Most reached 90. Mum, on the other hand, had a family history littered with cancer and premature deaths. Eve's death clock for her parents was set. Dad would last for ages and Mum would go first. As it happened, Dad got cancer and died in his seventies. Mum has gone on to become an active eighties adventurer. Eve's death clock for her parents was way off.

Paul's note:

I always thought I would not make Thursday (40). I have no idea why, but I did make it known to my ex-wife (no wonder we're no longer together—I was a pain in the arse). As it happens I made it past Thursday and she reflected that my clock was well and truly busted. I have seasonally adjusted my clock to a date I will now keep to myself. :)

Can anybody spare a dollar?

Ask any Defender their top three expenses and no doubt one of them will be food/groceries. There are all manner of ways to save on groceries: meal planning, buying online, using points to pre-buy vouchers, farmers markets…

These are all great ways to consider your spending, but think about how much effort we may make to save $10 on groceries, when we don't extend the same energy to save $10 off an electricity bill or a dress or a fridge—$10 is $10, but we treat money differently depending on where it's going.

Saving $10 at the supermarket feels good. You don't have to be a Defender to know that you spend a fair bit there. However, if you were buying a fridge for $1000 and managed to get $10 off it wouldn't have the same feeling of worth. Why? Well the percentage saving is one thing. A $10 saving on a $200 grocery bill is 5 per cent, while a $10 saving on $1000 is only 1 per cent. If someone offered you $10, no strings attached, would you gladly accept? If you found $10 in the street, that would be fantastic. You might even think of it as an 'omen' for your day or week, but the money would have a different 'tag' attached to it.

How we think about the same value of money is dependent on the context. However, $10 is $10 regardless of whether someone gave it to you, or you saved it on groceries or a fridge. Any money saved has value, regardless of where it came from.

One of the reasons why we don't always recognise this is that we categorise money into different 'categories' in our minds. We don't think about money for bills in the same way that we think about daily spending money. We categorise money based on random and subjective criteria. Often this is based on how we received the income (earnings from work are treated differently from an inheritance or gift card, for example). It can also be based on how we plan on spending the money (so savings for a holiday is separate from your debt).

A dollar is a dollar whether you saved it on your groceries or your next household bill. You still saved a dollar.

A dollar is a dollar whether you received it through work or as a birthday gift.

A dollar is a dollar whether you plan on spending it on a holiday or paying down debt.

Treating your money as though it's in arbitrary categories leads to placing less value on some dollars than others. Labelling money changes the way we spend.

A coffee a week

Regardless of their financial position, everyone has a sense of some of the obvious cost points in their life. For example, you know roughly how much a coffee costs you each day, or how much your rent or mortgage is each month. We use these as reference points for our spending, and marketers use them too.

Your Netflix or Spotify subscription is the same cost as a coffee a week. Your gym membership is the same cost as a coffee a day. A more expensive purchase of a furniture or technology item might be paid off monthly and you anchor it to other items you pay monthly such as rent or insurance, for example. In doing so it puts the cost in perspective. But it can also make the cost seem smaller than it really is.

Taking a moment to compare the value of something before purchasing it can help your brain to exercise its willpower muscles. Even a short delay between the impulse to buy and actually spending can help you change the way you think about the item. Would I rather have the awesome new pair of jeans for $100 or buy 25 coffees? Does this television feel like it's worth two weeks' pay/rent?

Time matters

Gym memberships and new year's resolutions. The two seem to go hand in hand each year. Gyms often have various payment options: annual, quarterly, monthly, for example. The data confirms that (most) people who pay for their membership annually attend more in the first month than in any other month. People who pay for their membership quarterly are most likely to attend when they pay each instalment, and people who pay monthly attend more consistently.

The further away we are from the time of payment, the more we're able to mentally discount the spend. The time between payment and consumption is significant. We also value things differently in the present from the future—that is, the longer into the future, the bigger the 'discount' we apply.

Be forgiving of yourself for slipping up and not attending. It's human. But don't think that you should give up. Changing the way you pay may help. Reframe the problem to be more positive ('I will' instead of 'I won't') in your mind and re-commit. Remember your goal. Repetition is one of the keys to successful habit change, so regardless of your payment schedule, re-commit for a month and value your future time and money.

We all hate losing

Ever lost something? Your wallet, a ticket to an event, got fleeced for some cash, gambled? We hate losing more than we enjoy winning. From small amounts to large, we're prone to obsess over losses more than we celebrate gains.

Like when you buy a ticket, and are sitting through a show, or a concert, and hating every minute of it. Maybe the seat is so bad it's just not worth it; the movie drags on, but you sit through the whole thing anyway. We don't want to feel like the money was 'wasted'. We can't bear the loss and want to restore it. Interestingly, we don't apply the same value to loss when it isn't our own money. Say you received tickets to a sporting event that you were looking forward to, but when the date arrived work was hectic, the weather was bad or you felt a bit poorly. The fact that someone else paid for the tickets would mean you're less likely to attend than if you'd paid yourself.

We apply this to many things that we buy and sell because we try to reduce the feelings of loss and regret, particularly when it's our own money. So shares or investments we bought that have since made a loss are hard to part with. Even the most experienced investor struggles to 'cut their losses' and professional investors have 'stop loss orders', which enforce selling at a particular value to try and counter the loss aversion. We're strongly affected by the price we purchased at.

This is a natural impulse that can be linked to our fight or flight response. Try reframing this in your mind. Take a minute. Pause. Think and plan. Don't be emotional about the decision.

It's complicated...

The world we live in requires people to have a high level of financial literacy. Despite the rise of websites to help people compare products such as insurance, loans or credit cards, the reality is that it's often difficult to feel confident in decisions around purchases, particularly financial products and services. Take health insurance: the factors to consider aren't only the premiums that you'll be required to pay periodically, but also the services offered; cover you'll receive; your understanding of government rebates; and also having some understanding of what services you predict you'll need. And that's not taking into account your own budget and the considerations that are required to manage competing priorities within your personal finances. Even the most educated consumer needs to spend a significant amount of time looking at all the variables to ascertain which product really is suitable. The result? Most people default to what they know or what their peers are doing, or they make a decision based on factors such as which product is mid-range. Or they do nothing.

Governments around the world have embraced financial literacy programs, making assumptions that educating people empowers individuals, that the appropriate levels of knowledge will assist in making the right decisions. In many cases this education is helpful. And certainly having access to the right information, calculators and tools when we need them is useful. However, despite all the educational opportunity, people still make decisions as human beings—imperfectly, inconsistently and influenced by emotion. Not to mention that Spenders don't turn up to financial education seminars, Slenders get frustrated and Defenders feel they're for money novices.

Our leaders have also tried to implement systems and research to understand some of the psychology behind our choices. The stuff that marketing has been doing or trying to do for many years.

Crime and money

Profiling and criminal psychology is accepted around the world as one of the methods used to solve and prevent crime. A fundamental aspect of this is to understand motivation: why criminals do things, their needs and values.

In recent years, governments around the world have begun using this same type of knowledge—behavioural science—to help make public services more cost effective and to help people make better choices. Psychology and criminal profiling have been around for a long time, with the biggest breakthroughs in criminal profiling happening after the FBI established its behavioural science unit in 1972. However, it wasn't until 2010 that the UK government set up one of the first departments to use this type of science as it relates to public policy.

Books, television, movies and podcasts in the crime genre continue to rate among the most popular with audiences looking for clues in behaviour to work out 'whodunnit'. In a small way, the audience is behaving like a detective, a behavioural scientist. Unfortunately, we're less aware of some of these behaviours in ourselves and in our everyday lives.

The UK government estimated that savings of over £300 million were made in an initial two-year period, with ongoing and additional savings each year, from its behavioural insights team. The unit continues today, and countries around the world, including Australia, Canada, Germany, India and Singapore, are imitating its success.

In 2017, Richard Thaler won a Nobel Prize for his work on 'nudges'. A nudge is a small suggestion or a positive influence on consumer choice. Nudges make it easier to make a decision: some are more obvious and transparent than others. In Thaler's work, nudges were intended to allow people to retain their freedom of choice, with the objective being to help people exercise better self-control, for example, when saving for a pension or choosing healthy food. This was probably the real turning point in the use of behavioural science in a more mainstream way around the globe.

So while it may be more widely known (and accepted) that governments are using behavioural science in relation to crime, they're also using this knowledge of how we make choices to suggest, or nudge, the general public in a particular direction. Assuming that the 'nudger' has your best interests at heart, that's okay. However, in the context of money, spending and marketing, understanding nudges and other aspects of behavioural science may help you make decisions.

Willpower, ego or habit?

There's debate over whether it's our ego, our willpower or simply long-formed habits that have the greatest influence on our decisions. Regardless of your opinion, here are a few tips for when it comes to your spenditude:

- Suppressing an urge can actually give it more power. Don't try to ignore it. Instead, notice your response, your breathing, and then make a decision to act.

- What are you using to control your stress? Gambling, smoking, shopping, drinking, eating or social media as a stress relief do not serve you well. Switch them out for walking, reading, meditation or music.
- Goals can be considered as things you will or won't do, and things that you want. Have consideration and focus.

If in doubt...

Have you noticed that restaurants, especially fancy ones, don't have dollar signs on menus any more? Sometimes they spell out the cost in words because dollar signs and numbers can increase our association to money and decrease our willingness to spend.

Next time you're choosing wine in a restaurant and you doubt your decision, maybe consider that a good thing. Trying to have your own mental anchors may help you to spend less, or not to spend. What wine spend is appropriate for you and your budget? How many hours' work do you have to do to buy that bottle? What else could you buy for the same price?

When you're buying a shirt and the second one is half price, being aware of the strategy the store is using and hesitating before spending can help.

Apply this to both small- and big-ticket items. Just because it's 'better than half price' doesn't mean you should buy it to get the 'deal'.

Say a designer handbag was $3000. It's on sale for $1000. Seems too good to be true. So cheap compared to the regular price. So tempting. But is $1000 okay for you to spend on this item? You could buy a month's (or more) groceries, a return flight to your next holiday destination or pay for your car insurance for a year. Okay, this may seem boring to some. You really want that handbag! But instead of anchoring the price tag to the original price, anchoring it to other things provides an opportunity for you to doubt, hesitate and consider your spend.

Defenders do this instinctively.

Show me the money

A dollar is a dollar regardless of how you saved it or received it. Try not to allocate spend based on the source of funds and treat this money differently. Tax returns, gifts and bonuses risk being spent more quickly than other 'earned' funds. Saving money for a holiday while carrying significant credit card debt doesn't make the best use of your dollars. If you receive money that you weren't expecting, think about where it can make the best financial impact.

Have a sense that asking for a discount, regardless of your purchase or spend, is worthwhile. Are you willing to hand over the extra money from your wallet? If you found it on the ground, would you keep it? Would the sales person be willing to hand it over to you? If not, then the discount request is valid.

Old money is not the same as new money

All in all, people would rather avoid losses than make gains of the same value. Losing $5 generates a much stronger response than receiving $5. People also prefer to maintain the status quo, even if changing circumstances would provide a better outcome or option. Sometimes change is hard.

Combine these two factors and we risk making decisions that aren't in our best interests. Say you bought a house or a car or some shares a few years ago and need to sell them today; the value will most likely be different from what you paid. If the value has decreased, then the emotional response is high. Losing money feels bad. Add to that our human tendency to consider the value of something we own to be higher than it really is, and we find it hard to make a decision. Status quo feels easier than a loss, even when we know selling is the right decision. So we're likely to do nothing.

It can help to be aware of this emotion and ask yourself, 'If I didn't own this, how much would I be prepared to pay for it?' In other words, it's a good idea to make these sorts of financial decisions based on today's prices. The price you paid doesn't always factor into making the best decisions in the present—especially if you feel you're making a loss.

Pain is relative

By increasing the pain of paying we can decrease our spend. Paying in cash is more painful than paying by credit/technology systems. Bringing the visual cues to our spend helps, whereas plastic and tech payments are somewhat hidden.

Pain is also decreased when we're multitasking and task switching. So online shopping while watching television isn't ideal and booking flights for your next holiday while you're at work won't help you focus on the best deal.

Subscription plans also work to this theory and decrease the pain. The first month is free; you're hooked and possibly forget to cancel the monthly payment. There's no immediate pain and there appears to be a discount.

Read the fine print:

I understand how I'm tricked into spending.

OVER TO YOU

Take five minutes for a coffee...

Ninety-nine per cent of personal finance blogs, books and education seminars tell you to stop drinking coffee. When you add up the cost of a daily coffee, it's $1500 a year, they say. And it probably is. But we say coffee can actually help you stop spending. So don't stop drinking coffee (but being aware of how much you spend is good).

Hesitating before spending is one of the best ways to curb instant gratification. Coffee helps. Whether you're considering purchasing something online or in person, first take a breath. Walk away for five minutes and make a coffee (or tea, or have a glass of water, or...). It's truly amazing the difference this can make in giving you time to bring to the front of your mind some of the concepts we've explained.

The best way to put this all into action is to use the 5-minute rule. So go make a coffee.

Chapter 8

What could possibly go wrong?

Where there's a will, there are relatives.

If we knew when we're going to die it would be so helpful for planning our finances. We could spend until we drop without fear of running out. Or if we knew we're going to live a long life we'd be far more focused on the long term.

Well, we don't know when we're going to leave this place. However, we do know that we'll leave one day. If we leave too early, without planning, it can cause a major kerfuffle for those left behind.

Defenders are much better (though not always perfect) at planning for contingencies such as premature departure from this earth, illness, losing your marbles and other door-closing moments that just happen.

Major organisations have a risk register. They identify potential risks, rate the risks' impact, consider whether they can insure against them and, if not, create a mitigation strategy. Why don't we do this for ourselves and our loved ones? Some Defenders do, but most people don't.

Forty-five per cent of Australians don't have an up-to-date will, the majority are uninsured and very few have a detailed estate plan in place. Why is this? There are many reasons, including apathy, a fear of addressing these depressing topics, a sense we might bring it on if we talk about it or simply 'I'll get round to it one day'. I'll WTF (Wait Till Friday).

This example shows what a risk register might look like.

My family risk register

Risk	Insurable?	Impact?	Mitigation strategy
I die too young.	Yes.	Kids' futures.	Ensure I have enough life insurance.
My partner dies or gets sick early.	Yes.	Less income. Kids' futures. Babysitting and care.	Have trauma-style insurance for my wife.
My Dad goes into a home	No.	Who funds it? Impact on estate. Sibling fights.	Ensure I have his Power of Attorney.

Here are some other risks to consider (the list could potentially be quite long so these are the top five):

- Lose job. No income.
- Get sick for the long term and my employer stops paying me.
- My kids need ongoing care when they're adults. If we both die, who looks after them?

- Parents getting old and need ongoing care. How do we pay for it?
- Investing in assets that don't produce enough of a return. Wasted opportunity.

A not-so-happy ending...

Fancy spending your whole life being a Defender and accumulating a wonderful nest egg and then you die too early, perhaps on Saturday.

You're in heaven or similar and looking down at the chaos you've left behind. Imagine that you overlooked setting up your final wishes: you didn't prepare a will.

Well, perhaps that's okay because surely your estate will go to your kids and their kids? Maybe, but perhaps not.

What you didn't take into account is the little matter of your first wife and your mad sister. They feel very much entitled to a slice of the action. You haven't talked to them for years—in fact, you dislike both of them in equal parts. Worse still, your ex ran off with your ex best mate. She's relishing the opportunity to claim her stake.

No-one can believe you forgot to write a will and the ex is building a strong case. Your very ex mate will also benefit. He sees you as the gift that keeps giving.

Your mad sister feels she's entitled as she's your only sibling.

Your grown-up kids are horrified and more than a little disappointed in you. What have you done, Dad?

You may ask, is this a bit far-fetched? Not really. When things go wrong they tend to be compounded by our complex lives.

We've enlisted the help of an expert to explain what could happen in this scenario. Donal Griffin is a lawyer and estate expert at Legacy Law (legacylaw.com.au).

Donal explains that, in the scenario above, anyone who falls into one of the following categories could make a claim on your estate when you pass away:

- a spouse or de facto partner
- a child, whether biological or adopted
- a former spouse
- a person who was dependent on you at the time of your death, including a grandchild who might have been a member of your household at some stage
- a person who was in a close personal relationship with you at the time of your death.

As you can see, these categories are open for debate. In your case, your adult kids and ex-wife could make a claim. Your mad sister would have to convince a court that her relationship was within these categories. In the experience of Legacy Law, people can 'try it on' and it can be expensive to disprove their claims in court.

Providing for the carer

Another example is old Grandpa. He's in a care facility and has a couple of investment properties in his will. He lives in another state and you don't see him that much. You know he's happy because he's always talking about Cristina, the carer: 'She is so nice.'

All of a sudden old Grandpa drops dead.

Fast track to the reading of the will. There's an unfamiliar person sitting next to you. You're sure that Grandpa has left his estate to you. You're his only grandchild and Nana went years ago.

As the will is read, the stranger in the room learns that she's receiving one of the properties. 'To my dear Cristina, what a wonderful carer you have been ...'

You're devastated.

Donal explains that this could happen. While children often take on the task of caring for their sick or frail parents and are usually taken into consideration in their will, some elderly people are predominantly looked after by a carer, who spends a lot of time with them in their final years. This results in carers receiving more than seems appropriate in the will — and this is quite common.

Donal says a recent case in New South Wales involved a carer who was left 100 per cent of her employer's estate in the final will. The deceased suffered from Alzheimer's disease for the last 10 years of her life. As she was estranged from her family, she developed a strong friendship with her carer and they frequently met socially. Family members who had been included in previous wills had been cut out. The court upheld the last will, but if there had been evidence that the relationship with the carer wasn't 'above board', the decision could have gone another way.

So, in Grandpa's case, Cristina could well get the lot.

The Defender hero

Let's look at another example, Siddarth. Siddarth is 42 (in his early Thursday) and married to Amy. They have three young kids and a big mortgage.

He is the main income earner and fit for his age. He heads off for his morning jog one day and drops dead.

It happens.

The only assets to give Amy are the house and the car. No inheritances and no insurance. Amy can't sell the house because then where would she and the kids live? She has enough grief to deal with, without uprooting their life and memories. What about the kids' education? She's distraught. The family is financially wrecked.

At the reading of the will the lawyer says, 'And to Amy and my three girls an equal share of $200 000 each; or to Amy the full $800 000 to ensure the kids get the education we dreamed of and also to keep you in the house. Pay off the mortgage.'

What? Amy thinks it's a mistake.

But no! Siddarth joined his work retirement fund, which included life insurance to the equivalent of five times his salary. He had the good sense to complete all the paperwork about beneficiaries. It was such a simple process, he forgot to tell Amy he signed it.

Let's go back to the reading of the will where Amy's thought of a mistake became a reality thanks to Siddarth's diligence in completing a simple process. You would be shocked to know that many Australians are not that diligent about taking notice of the insurance in their retirement fund—what signing those forms could mean to their family. (A big tip: check your fund. Be like Siddarth.)

This is Siddarth's greatest financial moment. In hindsight, he had a great Defender moment.

Making sure you're covered

Let's move away from death and consider other forms of insurance that can protect you.

Esther is single and a late Thursday. She was diagnosed with breast cancer and was very stressed. She had no partner and her parents had passed away. She was isolated.

She had income protection cover through work in case she needed to take a long-term absence, but she wanted to work to keep occupied. She was also concerned she might lose her job if she was away for too long.

Thankfully Esther had taken out trauma cover for $300 000. Upon diagnosis, she received the full payout and used most of it to pay out her mortgage and set up a nest egg in case she needed care.

There are many cases like Esther's where people are vulnerable. Trauma cover gets expensive as you enter Friday but in Esther's case it was a very smart decision. Paying off her mortgage gave her the peace of mind to know that she doesn't have to work forever.

What is trauma insurance?

Trauma insurance, sometimes called critical illness insurance, provides a lump sum of money in the event of a critical illness or injury. Trauma cover pays you an agreed amount to help with immediate medical and financial needs. It covers things like heart attacks, cancer or major injuries.

Enough of these tough stories, I hear you say. Okay…in a minute.

Defenders tend to think about risk more than Spenders and Slenders. They seek advice and ensure that big risks are mitigated.

We all owe our families the comfort of knowing that we've de-risked ourselves.

Families need to be more aware of the importance of writing wills and estate planning, including the need to update them when changes occur—especially unexpected ones! Poorly executed wills can cause long-term damage to families.

So that's a big risk. There are many others. Perhaps now is the time for you to develop that risk register!

Women's business

Do women face additional risks? The reality is that for the most part women earn less, women retire with less *but* women live longer. This is risky business.

The gender pay gap is now widely recognised and, although progress is slow in some areas, it's closing. Businesses are recognising that diversity (and not only gender diversity) at senior levels creates stronger companies. This is *not* about women vs men. (There are issues that need larger solutions and greater social change—but this is all too much to deliver in these pages.)

The reality is that women, in many cases, need some different strategies from men. Women have different career cycles than men. Their salaries peak earlier, and they have more career breaks and caring responsibilities; however, women are less likely than men to ask for a pay rise.

Women's money narratives are often different too. Women are more likely to engage in negative self-talk than men. Imposter syndrome, anyone? Women are also more likely to believe that they're 'bad at maths' and conform to the traditional and romantic ideals that women are better at 'caring professions'. In fact, the term 'math trauma' was coined back in 2016 to describe the impact of bad maths experiences at school and the impact this can have on long-term 'mental shutdown' as it relates to maths and numbers — and this includes money. Reality check: women are good at maths too!

Women are better investors

If we learn by experience, observations and detecting patterns in the world, then we assume that men are better at finance than women. The financial services sector has historically been significantly dominated by men and the observations and patterns we see demonstrate that this is a male industry. However, there are many stories of women being extraordinary leaders and outperforming their male peers.

In Iceland between 2008 and 2011, all the banks failed, except the one run by two women. In the aftermath of the global financial crisis, there was much discussion and speculation about the role of women in financial services, with a number of researchers agreeing that the situation would have played out very differently should women have had more representation in financial markets. The result in Iceland was significant, with women leading the charge to recovery, promising to inject values of openness, fairness and social responsibility.

Depending on which study you read, women are better investors because they:

- trade less, reducing losses
- prefer to buy underpriced stocks and sell overpriced stocks

- anticipate mis-pricing opportunities
- avoid risky trading activity
- are just not as excited about the stock market as men (making them more likely to stick to their plan).

Baby brain

All too often, taking maternity leave is like being placed in a dark cupboard in your workplace for up to 12 months—ignored in the corner with no contact, no updates and no training, and often no pay rise either. When the cupboard door opens 12 months later, there's an expectation that you know exactly what's been going on.

The reality is lots of women don't know how they'll cope with this new role of motherhood. Be the one to keep that cupboard door open, or at least ajar. If you're a woman on maternity leave, then advocate for yourself in a moment of change in your life. Keeping the door ajar might be a way to maintain a connection to your pre-parenthood self. Whether you're a career mum, an earth mum or a just-getting-by mum (or something else entirely), leaving an opening to connect with work while on leave could be the best thing for your financial future.

Entrapment

Yes, the world is changing, but there are still women financially entrapped by their partner. Be clear about the risk and mitigate it. If you rely on your partner's wage to pay the mortgage and something happens to him, are you going to be okay?

Have you ever taken out debt on behalf of a partner (or known someone who has)? Simply a phone contract or a small loan? Then the partner leaves and the other person is left with the debt. Or how about the wealthy woman stashing money somewhere because she's been cut off from all financial knowledge while her husband earns the big bucks and she raises the kids.

Financial entrapment is a real issue, and it's more common for women than men.

Janine's note:

Women sometimes seem to wear the mental load with anger, resentment and exhaustion. We're busy. All. The. Time. The result can be that we don't take the time to work out what our craft is, strengthen our skills and attract opportunity. Or we're too busy to see when that opportunity presents itself. All the busyness, the distraction and activity of being a wife, mother, daughter, friend, aunty and so on makes developing any sense of self hard.

Finding something in life that keeps you true to your values and works to your new money narrative is hard. Look out instead of in. What interests you and brings passion to your conversations? Be curious. Ask other women to share their stories. Take compliments. Accept help.

Living without anxiety around money could change the way you live. And remember, a relationship is not a financial plan.

Risk comes in all parts of our life. We walk past risk every day. Those who are Defenders tend to protect their assets (human and physical) and are aware of most risks. The best advice is to do what a good business does — that is, set up a risk register and review it regularly.

So how do you and your partner get on the same page with your finances? Read on …

Women have risks
that are unique
to them. Embrace
these risks and have
a plan to improve
your spenditude
by mitigating each
risk, one at a time.

Be prepared:

I understand my risks so I know what could possibly go wrong.

Chapter 9

Under the spreadsheets

Move over babe, I want to pull those spreadsheets up so we can have a good old chat. A chat that may well define the type of life we enjoy together. The type of chat that statistically may avert divorce. A chat that may influence our kids in a very positive manner.

The most taboo topic in relationships is discussing a common view on money values. It ranks below discussing postcodes we want to live in, the baby's name, comments on the dickhead uncle, houses we want to buy, holidays, kids' education and even a common view on being healthy together. Money values is a tough topic.

Imagine your partner is a Spender and you're a Defender or Slender. How do you possibly have a common money value system for your relationship? Remember Andrew in the restaurant (in chapter 1)? He pulled out his spreadsheet early in the relationship and, to his joy, his partner saw the value of being in the black. She saw a pathway that had never been so clear showing how to move from red to black. She was a Slender on a treadmill waiting for her Defender to turn up and share his plan. Unfortunately, this is the exception rather than the rule as far as these types of conversions are concerned. Why is money such a taboo topic? Perhaps we just don't know how to approach it effectively.

Paul's note:

I know in my circumstance (remember I was a Spender married to a Defender) I avoided the topic like the plague. It led to decisions being made under a compromise and we never really were on the same course as far as money was concerned. I regret this lack of planning as it wasn't good modelling for our kids, let alone our bank balances.

We need to talk about it

Before they marry or settle into a long-term relationship, couples have conversations around health, lifestyle, family, political beliefs, religion and the day-to-day stuff of life. They talk travel, dreams and goals, sport, music and movies, work, education and where they want to live. They probably talk about past relationships. Sometimes couples even attend 'pre-marriage' courses to help them navigate the ups and downs of their relationship. If money is discussed, it's usually at a superficial level, rather than sharing deep motivators and describing each other's spenditude. Understanding each other's attitude to money is the first step in 'couples awareness'.

Yet money features in the top three reasons why couples divorce, which are:

- infidelity
- money
- communication.

So if you want to avoid divorce, talk straight, share your spenditude and keep your pants on.

The declaration of independence

Let's talk a little about divorce. It's the most effective wealth-deflation strategy of all time. Both parties tend to be burned and it truly is a door-closing moment. If you plan to have no money by the weekend, get divorced.

The correlation between *no* money plans/values/strategies and divorce is absolutely real.

How many divorces could have been avoided if both parties had agreed to and applied a spenditude partnership plan? We asked Justin Hooper, a financial planner and expert on financial mediation for couples, including divorcing couples. He says, 'I would say almost all couples would end up with a much better financial outcome if they had addressed their underlying money beliefs and motivators.'

What is a spenditude partnership plan?

The first step is for both partners to write their goals into the days of the week (separately and jointly). What do we want Friday to look like? What's our weekend plan? How do we want our little Mondays to view our spenditude?

Then you identify to each other how you feel about these goals by rating each goal the scale below. Your priority is the 'must haves' (the rating 1s).

- Rating 1: Must have.
- Rating 2: Good to have.
- Rating 3: Would be nice.

Identify three things you have to do together to reach the must haves. Do a gap analysis—that is, the work required to achieve common goals and values.

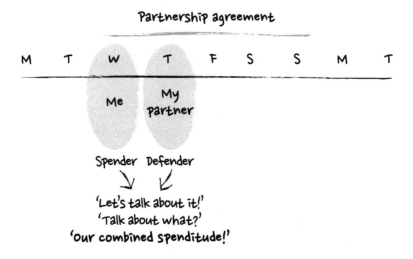

It's not really 50 per cent

Many couples have a bit of a fear complex that 50 per cent of marriages end in divorce. But that figure's not quite true.

The ABS reports that in 2017 in Australia there were 112 954 marriages and 49 032 divorces — that's about 43 divorces for every 100 marriages. However, these figures are for all marriages and divorces (regardless of whether it's the first or second or more) and the statistics also show that if you're marrying for the second or more time your chance of divorce is higher. Only about 30 per cent of first-time marriages end in divorce. The average length of time between marriage and divorce is 12 years. So does this mean the second timers continue to keep quiet about their spenditude?

We asked Justin ...

Why do you think money is one of the biggest causes of divorce?

Because money is so emotional. It exaggerates all sorts of feelings.

Money relates to our deepest anxieties and desires. It's the tool that people think they need to live the life they want. People believe that if they had more money they could close the gap between where they are and where they want to be.

But most people aren't aware that they have a 'frame of reference' through which they make all financial decisions. They have no idea that what they consider the truth about money is actually their fabrication. They are often not even fully aware of why they want money in the first place or what they are really giving up to get it. Each person is different and couples seldom have the same beliefs or deep motivators.

The tool of money exaggerates your emotions — the history/past that you bring to every decision. Throw into that some bad communication and fear and you get an explosion. I'm surprised there is not more divorce.

What tips would you give to couples trying to start a spenditude conversation?

Couples need to accept that they are not trying to do therapy. Equally, it's not about judging good or bad beliefs — it's simply about gaining a deeper understanding. As a result, the most important characteristic of the conversation is to be inquisitive. Always ask from a place of curiosity and kindness. Asking about the 'why' or 'so what' helps keep moving through. It helps us to grasp the messages that you/they were picking up and learning as a child. If you judge, the conversation will not be beneficial.

Don't interrupt; be a good listener. We each have our own unique experiences. Be open to hearing their experiences. We are all different; judgement doesn't belong with this kind of openness. Tune in with your whole body and don't be distracted. Let them tell you their story.

Sometimes, it can be better if the conversation is facilitated. Especially if there are some communication issues.

How does this help couples?

There can be massive differences in the way couples do things. Awareness is their saving grace. In coming together with awareness they can try and satisfy both people — not by compromising, but by looking for an elegant solution that takes the pressure out of the system. It can give people what they want and what they need.

In couples that have been married for a long time this type of conversation can take away some of the blame. The conversation is simply a conversation, without criticism or judgement.

In couples that are starting out it can help see where there is trouble ahead. It can also help you have gratitude for the things that you do have.

Is there anything else that we should know?

If done well, these conversations are enormously liberating. However, when partners have known each other for a long time, it can be difficult to have them without a facilitator. The ideal is someone who has been through a process like this themselves and who is simply trying to help you live your life rather than someone who has any preconceived ideas.

Those money narratives and *why* factors (from chapters 4 and 5) can have a huge impact on the way we deal with money. The complexity of combining two people's stories—which may differ wildly—means that this conversation really is essential.

We all have memories of incidents in our childhood— sometimes minor things—that affected us emotionally and create beliefs in adulthood. If you mowed the lawn or washed the car for money every week, then perhaps those thoughts are around 'working hard for money'. If your partner had experiences where large sums of money came and went, they may believe it's unnecessary to stick to a budget and this can create enormous conflict.

Another common childhood influence around money is where one parent, often Dad, worked and Mum stayed home. This could translate to a belief that 'if you don't work, you're trapped' and that can influence behaviour, habits and attitudes, which can have a profound impact on your relationship. Asking yourself, and your partner, if the beliefs are supporting or limiting you is important. It's not only childhood experiences—it could be other life events that need considering.

But remember that the money narrative is only the part above the water. The deep motivator—the *why* under the surface—is never about money. Money is the enabler. Those deep *why* factors, the values and motivators, are linked more to who you are—to those feelings deep in your heart/mind/tummy. They could be about living a life of adventure and creativity—being the mother/father you always wanted to have, or something else entirely, but not about money. This is the theme in your life—your 'treasure'.

Let's get back under that spreadsheet...

Relationships don't just work out, they need some steering. A lack of effort and poor communication around money is not the best way to start, or to continue. So how do you start talking about money with your partner?

What's important to you?

Back in the late 1990s George Kinder (author of *The Seven Stages of Money Maturity*) came up with three questions that were intended to provide clarity about what's important to you. Asking these questions separately and then sharing the answers is a powerful exercise.

1. If you were financially secure and money was no issue, what would you be doing right now?

This is the big dream. All financial constraints removed. It's hard to clear your mind of financial constraints. You might be surprised by your own answers and your partner's. Try to keep the doubt and negativity out.

2. If you only had five years to live, what would you change in your life?

This is a question of time, not health. Assume that you have no health issues, but you know time is limited. This question is not about unlimited funds. It's right now, for your current situation.

3. If you found out you were going to die tomorrow, what would you regret not doing?

It's not long enough to change anything big. What have you always wanted to do that you will miss out on?

Focus on having a conversation with your partner. Relationships fail when we don't do this. It brings awareness. It reduces judgement and blame. It has the potential to open up pathways for our journey and to avoid door-slamming moments.

Money in the container: when a Defender marries a Defender

Rick is married to Kate. They're both early Thursday (forties), no kids, good jobs that pay well. They have worked in Australia, the UK and Asia.

They're quite an independent couple. They're both Defenders.

Rick and Kate have never had joint accounts. They decided early on that they don't want to know what the other is spending, but believe that they should allocate and share expenses in a fair manner. This allocation is done monthly and is determined by their incomes.

They have a spreadsheet that has both their incomes recorded on it. They use this information to allocate expenses based on percentage of their incomes. If Kate earns more, she pays more for all combined expenses (rent, groceries, bills). No questions asked.

Their discretionary spending is not shared. Holidays are joint or separate. If joint, it's recorded as a shared expense.

Kate believes this system creates a sense of independence. 'We trust each other and have similar views on spending so there are rarely any surprises.'

Rick and Kate don't understand the concept of a joint account and they feel it would cause too many disputes. Rick believes their model is becoming the norm now and has seen friends operating the same way. He believes it's probably a sign of the times, where we all seek some form of independence.

Rick and Kate have some other interesting habits.

(continued)

Money in the container: when a Defender marries a Defender *(cont'd)*

Rick puts all his change into a container. Kate sees this as funding dry cleaning — in particular ironing of his shirts. In her mind, dry cleaning and ironing are a bit of an extravagance, therefore there's a little bit of guilt that they outsource something they could do themselves. The change container takes away the guilt because the change is seen as money otherwise wasted so they make it work for them.

The 1 percenters

Rick is a real Defender with some useful tips that he and Kate practise all the time. He loves the 1 percenter rule and shares it with us now.

Rick's view on money is that the 1 percenters make a huge difference over time. One percenters are the smaller things that add up over the long haul and can have a huge impact if we take them into consideration. Big 1 percenters make an immediate impact.

An example is negotiating lower fees when buying a home and negotiating lower interest rates by shopping around. These are big 1 percenters as their value over time is large.

Little 1 percenters are things like using a reusable coffee cup and saving 50 cents per coffee. It all adds up. Both Rick and Kate strongly believe in the rule of 1 percenters.

Other Defender habits

Kate and Rick are very conscious of not 'keeping up with the Joneses'. This isn't something they do. They don't like the concept and don't care if they're out of step with popular culture.

Another example is 'Eatigo' (an online reservation platform for restaurants in East Asia). Rick has subscribed to this app and gets up to 50 per cent off meals at restaurants in many countries. We've seen first-hand how much joy he gets out of selecting a restaurant and then experiencing the 50 per cent discount.

Finally, we leave Rick and Kate considering a flight to Ireland. They can afford an upgrade and the flight is long; however, there's no way they would waste money on that. It's just not in their Defender DNA.

Single and under those spreadsheets

Demographically, single people are a growing part of our community. People are taking longer than ever before they marry or are choosing not to marry. Living alone is becoming more popular in developed countries. In 2017 Canada saw more people living in single-person households than ever before and other developed countries are experiencing similar changes.

For a long time, society has placed pressure on people to marry, but studies from Switzerland, the United States and Germany have all found that single men and women can enjoy great health outcomes, and happy and fulfilled lives. The scientific evidence is there. Married people don't experience higher self-esteem levels, better sex lives or better overall health.

According to the 2016 Australian census data, one in four households is a single-person household (that's about two million people). Fifty-five per cent of these are female. This has been slowly but steadily increasing. The Bureau of Statistics is predicting that this will rise by up to 65 per cent by 2036, meaning an estimated 4.3 million more single-person households. And the Australian Institute of Family Studies predicts that by 2026, single-person households will outnumber traditional nuclear families.

There are many benefits to single living. Financial independence might be one of them. Perhaps a more limitless life where choice is not dictated by others. The debate rages on about the costs of single living compared to a living as a couple — a two-person household can share the cost of living (rent, bills) whereas a person living alone has to manage these expenses alone (although they only have to manage their own spenditude and not negotiate with another person).

Depending on your spenditude and income, single living can be a different path to negotiate as you work through your days of the week.

Singles need to self-assess rather than sharing with someone. This can be a trap and those who share with trusted advisers or friends tend to feel more comfortable with their plans.

Italy for the win!

Ali is enjoying late Thursday (forties). She has no kids and has three other friends in a similar situation. These four Thursday women have an agreement to buy four villas in the same neighbourhood in the south of Italy (somewhere around the Amalfi coast) and to live there when they finish work. Their pact is to look after each other as they enter their weekend and beyond. They have even developed a financial strategy to support each other.

It sounds a bit out there until you reflect on its merit.

> They know they won't have kids to support them in their 'next week' so they will look after each other.
>
> 'Why in the south of Italy?' we asked.
>
> Ali responded, *'Perché no?'* (Why not?)
>
> We love it!

Spenditude on your dating profile?

Single and out there? Perhaps we should be more open about our spenditude on our dating profiles.

- Photo ✓
- Age ✓
- Long walks on the beach ✓
- Spenditude ✓

'I have a GSOH, like to eat out, travel, read and have fun. I am fit and young at heart and, most importantly, I'm a Defender.'

Bingo!

Swipe right.

All this talk of being under spreadsheets can lead to ...

Little Mondays. Ankle biters. Kids.

Can we identify spenditude in our kids? What type of behaviour do we want them to have? How can we raise more Defenders (or at the very least, fewer Spenders)?

Kids learn in two key ways:

- through observation
- through detecting patterns in experiences.

That is, kids learn more through what they see than what they hear. So children make up their own minds about everything from what they perceive to be true—and that includes money.

Think about the rules of childhood:

- Don't run with scissors.
- Don't play with matches/plastic bags/money.
- Don't talk to strangers.
- Share. Listen. Play nicely. Don't fight. Tell the truth.

What's the point? In the context of learning, some rules are more easily observed (adults don't run with scissors) and there's likely to be consistency in experience (Mum/Dad always stops me from running with scissors) and, depending on age, you can explain the consequences (scissors = negative). However, other rules are much more complex for children to understand, particularly when they observe adult behaviour. Don't talk to strangers—but Mum had a chat with that lady in the supermarket.

Lots of people tell their kids not to play with money because it's dirty. This isn't a good framework in which to commence a relationship with money. Believing money is dirty starts the taboo. As we move to a more cashless society, money is hidden from sight and replaced with tapping plastic. What does a child notice? Signs that say 'sale' perhaps? Advertisements targeted to grab their attention? Santa? Gift cards? A friend's new car?

Think clearly about a small child's view of shopping, money and spending...

- Fill the trolley with food, tap a card, phone, or even a watch or ring, and walk away with the goods.
- Pick an object on the internet and have it magically appear at your house a few days (or even a few hours) later.
- Lunch orders from the school canteen just happen, as Mum/Dad organised them online.
- Bills don't arrive in the mail anymore, so there's likely to be little conversation around the price of water, electricity and so on.

Kids are always taking in information—even if it's not what you're trying to get them to learn. And in the same way that we can't expect our kids to eat broccoli if we don't eat it, we can't expect our kids to learn good spenditude if we're displaying something different from what we're trying to teach them.

How do we identify spenditude in kids?

Start the narrative with your partner around 'What type of behaviour do we want our kids to have?' If it's Defender, then work out how you can make it happen.

As we've already discussed, the old adage is true: kids don't hear, they see. Demonstrate good spenditude and they may follow early. Teach them the magic of compound interest before they're 10. They'll get it if you explain that Albert was the smartest man on the planet and he believes it's MAGIC. Kids love magic.

Some tips to get your kids focused in an unfocused world:

- Mindfulness meditation can start around age six so have them listen to a five-minute meditation daily. Not brainwashing but gently influencing their own little emerging narrative.

- Get them involved in helping others. There are many great organisations that provide support to disadvantaged kids.
- Show them the Good Return website where they can lend money through microfinance to a person with less who is trying to be a Defender.
- Get them managing some of their own money and making their own mistakes.
- Talk about it—explain how the money got to the ATM; how you paid for the online shopping that arrived.
- Teach them about presence, not presents.
- Delay gratification.
- Set goals and help them succeed (pick things that are achievable at first).
- Explain your own choices: why are we making this purchase (how does it align to our family values)?

Are Julie's kids spoiled?

Julie is a Defender living in a reasonably affluent suburb of Melbourne. Julie lives in an apartment with her two kids and partner. They're doing okay, but aren't as financially advanced as some of the people in their network.

At the beginning of each school year the list of stationery comes home: pencils, notebooks, glue and the like. Julie and her kids diligently stop at the store to get the required items. Despite having plenty of pencils, the kids demand new ones. Julie is hesitant. She's a Defender and knows they have some at home. They really don't need new ones.

Julie feels that she has two choices. Buy the new pencils to keep the peace or enter into the conversation about recycling, money and other people who aren't so fortunate.

Earlier that day, Julie had overheard a conversation between mums in the school playground that focused on another family's wealth and their fancy home. Upon hearing this, Julie realised that her kids were starting to observe things around them and assume that many people lived in a large home with a pool, plenty of toys and a couple of cars in the garage. This was becoming their 'normal' despite the fact that they lived more simply. In comparison, the pencil matter was a simple choice.

While the pencils may not make that big of a difference, Julie opened up a conversation with her kids about money. In paying attention to what her kids were observing, and therefore learning, she was able to create a new dialogue. She may not be able to influence the daily interaction and observations that her children have, but she can help her children bring a Defender's value lens to purchases.

Yes, Julie's lucky. While Julie's kids may learn some lessons through observation, she is aware.

Her own habits as a Defender may rub off. The pencils may be a simple experience that's remembered.

So let's break away from money being a taboo topic and start sharing our money stories. Not boasting about how much we have but how we go about our relationship with money. We can all learn a lot from each other.

In the next chapter we think about having a bit on the side—but not the kind that leads to divorce (and more Mondays). No, earning money while we sleep is the goal.

Share and learn:

I discuss money with my loved ones so we have a common view of our spenditude.

Chapter 10

A bit on the side (and the future of work)

Earning income while you sleep. Now that's a plan!

There has always been access to a bit of income on the side. Back in the day that was mowing lawns, doing stuff no-one else wanted to do, hospitality and seasonal labour. Now, there's a whole world of extra income out there. It even has a name: the side hustle is here.

side hustle: 'a way to make extra cash that allows you flexibility to pursue what you're most interested in'
Source: entrepreneur.com

The idea of having a single job for life and following a career ladder within one organisation is increasingly unlikely. There are shifts in our demographic makeup and our economic environment, as well as numerous social shifts taking place (think about our ageing population, more single-person households, urbanisation, technological influence, etc.).

Is the side hustle a way to get ahead? Are all side hustles equal?

This phenomenon is attractive to Defenders, Spenders and Slenders. It has something for everyone.

Defenders see it as a way to not waste resources but to put them to work. Whether that's your time, effort or something you possess. Money coming in while you get on with your life. Money while you sleep if you get it right.

Slenders see it as a way to make ends meet. Many Slenders are Uber drivers as they see this as a chance to earn a bit more so they can manage their finances better (maybe you won't have to worry about driving strangers around half the week if you improve your spenditude).

Spenders. Well, they see this as fuel for their lifestyle needs or perhaps to bridge the gap so they can pay off bills.

A pair of hustlers

There are two types of side hustle. One uses high personal exertion and the other very little exertion (they earn money while they sleep). Let's explore them in more detail.

Personal exertion side hustles

For this, you'll need time in your week and, more than likely, a car. Top of the list is ride-share driving. Uber is the category leader in this field.

We've spoken to many Uber drivers and most report that the money isn't that good. However, the hours are okay and flexible ('whenever I feel like it'). It's really interesting to find out the backstory of each driver. We've met mums who want a break from being home with the baby, men who retired too early and are bored, a grandmother who loves a chat, many graduates looking for extra cash, business owners looking to top up their cashflow troughs, a real estate agent who uses it to expand his prospecting network, a neighbour who uses it to pick up people on the way to work so her parking fee is funded by the fare, a doctor who wants to talk to healthy people, a prostitute (true story) who wants to meet men who want a conversation, many researchers who are working on books or theses (not us — well, perhaps a little), musicians who can work the good hours where surging prices exist, several executives who have been retrenched, and people who just need the money and have a car.

It's not difficult to get started and the app that drives activity is quite easy to master. It's without doubt the poster child of side hustles for those who have time and a car. The downside is the hours of personal exertion required. For some it's their job, not a side hustle.

Of course, the extension to share rides is the food delivery industry. Wow, has that taken off! What's different is you don't need a car. A bicycle or motorbike will do just fine. With a bicycle you're also getting fit.

Second in the personal exertion category is the various job board apps. Airtasker is an example. You can source almost any skill on this app. It's amazing how efficiently it works for both parties. It's an absolute no brainer if you have particular skills and resources. From furniture delivery, picture hanging, pool cleaning or walking someone's dog, to IKEA assembly, photography, IT support and house cleaning. The best providers are very efficient. They respond to your request in minutes and ask good questions.

This side hustle can be quite lucrative. We saw an article the other day about a guy who earned $170 000 per year from Airtasker. He completed 172 painting jobs for about $1000 per job. Yes, a very busy man (if each job took two days, then he only got 21 days off in the whole year!). A great return on his effort. Lots of exertion, but also good money.

There are so many apps that cater for specific skills that just about all of us could sign on to be a provider. Other skills catered for include music-related services: musicians for hire, agents for musicians for hire and musical equipment for hire. For professionals there are more specific apps; for example, ones for creative types, lawyers, architects, engineers and accountants.

Amazon Flex is another side hustle that combines your time with the enormous power of Amazon behind you. You sign up to their app and then make between $18 and $25 per hour delivering packages for Amazon.

Very-little-exertion side hustles

The leaders in side hustles requiring less personal exertion are Airbnb and other home-sharing apps. Once again, this is an amazing concept where you create an income from space in your house that you don't use. There are so many stories about how people have created a significant income from Airbnb listings. It's relatively simple to get started and you control who you allow into your home based on a trust rating system — and there's no personal exertion.

Joanne makes it work

Joanne is a flight attendant working the international routes. She flies out for four- to six-day shifts, so she's away from home for reasonably long periods of time. Joanne is a Defender who wants her assets to be working for her.

Joanne has listed her apartment on Airbnb. Her flight schedule is embedded into the availability calendar and she hardly has a night when her apartment isn't earning her income.

Joanne describes this as being 'savvy'. She's away working, and earning an income, and her place is also earning her money while she's flying around the world.

Joanne outsources the administration and cleaning so there's *no* exertion required.

Another example of a side hustle with little exertion is social media. By creating an Instagram following you become an influencer who has the power to endorse products and services. In return you receive contra services or real cash. A friend has a cute-looking cat and she started posting her on Instagram. Within a year she had over 18000 followers. Yes, she worked it hard early, posting cat phrases that matched the pose. She now earns significant income by placing products next to the cat's photos on Instagram. She knows exactly what photos work and what products will be attracted to her messaging. A large social media following is real currency for her.

There are many other side hustles and if you think about it the current environment is perfect for side hustling. As a community we tend to outsource more than ever. Busy is the new black. With no time, we tend to look for alternatives and this is where the side hustle is strongest.

Consider a skill you may have or an asset you possess that you could put to work. Go check out your pets to see if any of them are Insta-worthy! Just imagine earning money without too much exertion and then overlay being a Defender, where you turn that money into financial freedom. The choice is yours.

For retirement and the side hustle see chapter 11. There are some amazing side hustles for those who have wisdom and time.

Side hustles to consider

- Renting out your property
- Driving (including food and goods delivery or ride sharing)
- Fitness training or coaching
- Consulting or freelancing
- E-commerce or drop shipping
- Tutoring or teaching
- Reselling items online
- Babysitting
- Caretaking
- Computer repairs
- Housecleaning
- Household repairs and jobs
- Landscaping or gardening
- Survey taking
- Photography or videography
- Making or selling crafts
- Language translation
- Pet sitting or dog walking
- Blogging
- Mystery shopping
- Virtual assistant
- House-sitting
- Transcribing
- Proofreading

- Graphic design
- Social media marketing

The gig economy

the gig economy: 'a labour market characterised by the prevalence of short-term contracts or freelance work as opposed to full-time work'
Source: HR Review

Living and working in the gig economy means taking more responsibility for your personal finances—and your dreams shouldn't be worth more than your sleep (see chapter 2).

There seems to be a belief that being part of the gig economy is a luxurious lifestyle: be your own boss, take breaks when you want them, choose which gig to accept. And that guy who lives in Bali and spends summer in Spain makes it public and glamorous online because he's 'totes in control' of the work he takes on, isn't he? But is the perception different from the reality? Is it actually easy to live the dream by receiving an unstable income with no sick pay or other protection that comes with more traditional jobs?

The trend to outsource or move things offshore began quite a few years ago, often as a means of reducing costs. It hit some industries harder than others. Take cleaning, for example. People used to be employed by an organisation and received all the benefits of being an employee. Now organisations outsource their cleaning to a company that then outsources the labour. Usually, the person doing the work has none of the protection that comes with regular income and employment, such as sick leave and annual leave.

The gig economy extends to not just outsourcing departments and roles but breaking down the tasks and outsourcing them to anyone in the world (depending on the requirements) who is able to perform the gig.

While the gig economy may bring great opportunities, from the perspective of spenditude it's not really a long-term solution for our finances or wellbeing. Take Uber drivers, for example. They probably earn less than cab drivers and, as we've seen, it's a pretty high-exertion gig. You have to put in time and effort every hour that you're driving.

And this extra exertion — especially if it's your second job — is possibly disrupting your sleep (see chapter 2), which will disrupt your overall wellbeing. Perhaps we should put all the extra effort into advancing and expanding our skills instead. Or engaging in a side hustle that allows us to focus on our passions. If you feel that your real passion isn't sustained through employment, a side hustle can be a great way to indulge and make some extra cash.

Anyone with a great idea and some sales and marketing knowledge can access software, build a website and create a front end for their business with the back end being handled by software and outsourced suppliers. A great idea and a little spare time can result in a great little business. Work hard or work smart (or work hard and smart).

Our shifting workforce

The future of work is being discussed and debated across the world and the technological revolution that has changed industries is fuelling the debate about what the workforce will look like in the future. Add to that artificial intelligence (AI), which is predicting our consumer behaviour. Sometimes we don't learn from history. It's worth going back to the 1970s and imagining how the future of work was discussed then. Is it same-same but different? Or just very different now?

Back then, the future of work was more around the demographics within the workplace. Women's roles in the workforce were changing rapidly and students entering the workforce were more educated. And of course, automation via computers and technology was just beginning to make an impact. All big changes, and the word 'gig' was something that a musician had at a club. We were cynical, and, for some, very concerned this new world would leave traditional jobs behind. Sound familiar? But what happened was that more jobs were created to suit the consumerism of the time. Is it just the same now?

Talk of the gig economy and agile workforce could have happened back then as it does today. So where are we heading if everything old is new again? We asked an expert who designs employee behaviour by creating the carrot (not the stick). He designs incentive plans across industries.

Jairus Ashworth is a partner in Aon's Reward Practice in Australia and New Zealand. Jairus has been learning about the gig economy, talking about it and consulting to large organisations about our changing workforce for over 25 years.

Jairus says...

> I think that the move towards a 'gig economy' is not really that great for most people. Permanent employment came about because humans have a fundamental need for security, safety, predictability — remember Maslow's hierarchy? These things are at the bottom for a reason.
>
> Otherwise, unpredictable income means that we need to move around for work, take what is offered and risk getting stuck in a bit of a cycle. People who are working in less developed countries that have less predictable income are stuck in a trap of subsistence living. This is not the way anyone in that situation wants it to be; they are looking for more stability.

The other reason a gig economy is not great is that it can take us away from social networks, our tribe so to speak. Most people get value out of that part of employment.

What about in more corporate or professional types of jobs?

Well, I can't ever see a gig economy where a company hires a CEO for temporary work but there are parts of corporate roles that can be broken down. You could argue that doctors and surgeons are part of the gig economy. Anything can be broken down — you can gig economy almost anything.

Where the gig economy doesn't work is in roles that are about relationships and that rely on personal service. The tasks might get outsourced but the analysis and support that the process needs stays.

Think about human resources: you can outsource the recruitment, the learning and development, but someone still needs to choose the supplier, manage the decisions, and select what is being funded and how much is being spent. The actual work might be 'gigged' but someone still needs to decide what to do and how to do it.

Human insight cannot be outsourced. We might outsource the 'doing' part of work but the human-to-human service, analysis and insight is still here.

How do you think the traditional career ladder is changing?

Companies are seeing more value in the sideways moves. This is particularly apparent in tech industries. Moving your knowledge across the business has traditionally not allowed for a pay increase but more and more we are seeing that companies are recognising the insight that comes with this type of role change. The companies that are producing the best results are welcoming this lateral career 'matrix' and rewarding it financially. Someone who has worked in multiple areas of the business has more ability to connect and innovate.

There's been a change in the workforce. Organisations are looking at things differently and so must we. The roles of the future will require you to have good influencing skills, be able to tell a story and negotiate. In fact, a recent LinkedIn survey confirmed this, stating that the top skills of the future are creativity, persuasion and collaboration. Humans interacting with humans. Who would have thought?

It seems the career ladder is a thing of the past. The Foundation for Young Australians predicts that we will move to an era where we have 17 different employers across five different careers. We'll step sideways and cross industries more than ever before. Of course, there will still be a place for people with deep expertise, and those people may provide the glue that allows for more lateral moves. For people with transferable skills who are willing to learn, starting in the middle with a bit of extra education is becoming more common. Companies today are not as loyal as they used to be, and neither are employees.

The onus is firmly on the individual: you need to keep yourself employable. Although it's predicted that the future of work will change dramatically, there are core human skills that are sustainable and will be even more valued in the future. What's clear is, we must continue to learn. To freshen up our knowledge so we're 'future ready'. No-one will do this for us.

The digitalisation of university courses and degrees means courses from universities and colleges all over the world can be accessed from anywhere. Upskill, keep learning, be proactive.

So what does all this have to do with your spenditude? We're living in changing times and what worked for our parents may not work the same for us. Being able to have more focus on your financial situation is a skill that will assist you to manoeuvre through the changing landscape. Many of us will jump on the gig train and that train needs a heightened spenditude.

If you don't ask, the answer is always no

Negotiating your job, salary or bonus could make a big difference to your income.

Do Defenders do more homework than Slenders or Spenders before negotiating a new job or bonus? If so, what do they do that makes them feel as though they have a good deal? For corporate-type roles how many of us research the company to see whether it made a profit last year (a lead indicator of the bonus pool)? Do we ever investigate the salary range or even know how to do this?

Imagine if you had information about the salary range bands and the bonus pool payout when you went in to negotiate a job. Imagine getting paid more just by being prepared.

Spenders tend to ask for the highest pay because they consume all of it. However, in many cases they're ill prepared.

By self-identifying your spenditude before applying for a job, you have a better understanding of what you're looking for. Perhaps employee benefits will be more effective and valuable to you if you understand their true worth. Many organisations struggle to communicate benefits that have real value.

Benefits with a financial value

- Online university courses (can be discounted or preferred conditions if offered through your organisation)
- Life insurance and income insurance. If there's a group scheme it's likely the premiums are less than retail and the terms tend to have higher limits on not having to have medicals (extremely valuable if you're uninsurable)

- Working from home. WFH is becoming a benefit. One day a week at home reduces the cost of getting to and from work
- Wellbeing benefits like access to fruit, yoga or a personal training course
- Access to financial education
- Employee assistance programs providing counselling at no cost
- Retirement funds that offer low fees and access to lower-cost investment options
- If you're on a roster, knowing that it's well planned can be a huge benefit
- Discounted products or services.

Spenders may be willing to work double shifts for extra money. Their spenditude creates a short-term focus and the salary or potential to increase income is a big part of their decision. But offer a Spender more money for their retirement fund and they're just not interested.

Slenders may be willing to take a pay cut if their roster is well planned in advance or they have the flexibility they need to meet the demands of the other parts of their life.

Defenders are looking at the bigger picture. They're looking deep into the organisation and seeing where there's more value. What employee benefits can I access that will add value to my employment income? If pay rises remain stagnant, benefits have to become the new 'pay rise'. Defenders are all over benefits.

Personalised rewards

A few companies are beginning to recognise the need to give more choice in incentive design. The one-size-fits-all approach to remuneration and incentives doesn't always work. In the same way we expect our music and entertainment subscriptions to send recommendations based on our usage, it's important to acknowledge that Spenders, Slenders and Defenders will be attracted to different types of incentives and benefits.

For Spenders, it's probably short term and more focused on cash. Spenders don't want a free gym membership; they would rather have more cash.

Higher contributions to a retirement fund are more likely to draw the attention of Defenders, and some Slenders. This type of benefit doesn't change someone's spenditude.

Organisations that have a one-size-fits-all approach may be limiting their candidate pool or risking turnover by not considering who their benefits plan suits.

Are reward programs geared towards Defenders?

Enhancing your spenditude can help you find the value in company benefits. It's your spenditude that drives choices. Historically, we have believed that incentives being centred around company performance steered behaviour, but this is not the case. HR and executives within an organisation need to consider what spenditude could mean for incentive design and reward programs. Long or short term, cash or other forms of reward will appeal to different spenditudes.

Jobs for today's Mondays (tomorrow's Wednesdays)

Some experts are suggesting that kids born today will be working in roles that are yet to be invented and that up to 40 per cent of current jobs won't exist in 10 or 20 years.

As technology has changed the way we communicate and influenced our social interactions, it's predicted that technology will also affect our career paths into the future.

The Foundation for Young Australians suggests that transferable skills, such as problem solving, communication and teamwork, along with an optimistic mindset could be two of the key factors for young people when seeking employment.

This landscape has been described as the fourth industrial revolution.

Next up: retirement could kill you or may cause you to go mad. It's an outdated construct that gets a complete makeover in chapter 11.

Passive income:

I'll look at new ways of earning income to take control of my future.

Chapter 11

Rewirement

The term 'retirement' is out of date; it's boring to anyone pre-Friday (fifties) and to some it's a bullsh*t term. It's not healthy for a person to stop working altogether. They'll go mad first and then die early.

We heard this fact from a prominent Sydney psychiatrist. He said that the concept is flawed and the term 'retirement' should be—well—retired!

Retired—re-tyred. Is it the same thing? We drive on tyres all week and then we get to the weekend and need to re-tyre or re-tread them.

So is it *retyrement* we seek?

Or is it *re-wirement*? We like that term. We need to constantly be re-wiring ourselves for the future. So perhaps we'll say, 'I'm constantly planning my rewirement.' That will mean your rewirement starts *now*—not many years into the future. That way, every day of the week is a good time to plan for the future. For example, a Tuesday (twenties) could re-wire by focusing on getting in the black by the time they hit Wednesday. Thursdays could re-wire by paying down debt by Friday so they can start focusing on their life, rather than their constant worry about debt. Saturdays re-wire by creating little side hustles.

The old way to retire

My (Paul's) dad worked for the Post Master General (PMG), which became Telecom, which then became Telstra, Australia's telecommunications giant. A 45-year career. He paid extra units into his retirement fund from mid Tuesday. He retired on the stroke of midnight Friday (at 60). He always said that those extra units would come in handy one day. Lucky bugger has now outlived the actuarial calculations. He's now into his next Tuesday (90s). Thirty years (three days) of drawing down those extra units of retirement money.

I do think, though, that he's one of *The Last of the Mohicans* (a 1993 movie about a tribe that was becoming extinct). By that I mean that he worked 45 years uninterrupted, stopped working for a big organisation on Friday night and has enough in the bank until — well — forever. He's had no income worries in three decades.

We, on the other hand, live in very different times.

In the 1970s, the life expectancy of a man was 73. Sunday morning. Men made up the majority of the Australian workforce. The three main occupations were manufacturing (making stuff), building and related trades, and white-collar jobs. The white collars had the best deal. Their bodies were in reasonable shape when they collected their gold watch at 65 (Saturday lunch). A combination of the aged pension and savings funded their retirement. Most only needed less than 10 years of funds due to their life expectancy. Gone by Sunday night.

The blue collars worked hard and their bodies were ready for retirement long before Saturday lunch (65). Many didn't last long into their weekend.

Women were a smaller part of the workforce and they had a different retirement age as they were expected to live to around 78—later on Sunday.

What's changed?

Fast forward to now. The workforce isn't so homogeneous. There's a shared gender workforce for many occupations. Gender pay gap is still an issue; however, it's closing slowly. The workday isn't 9 to 5 anymore and the top three most popular occupations are nothing like in the 1970s. Life expectancy has blown out to 84 for males and 87 for females—about one full day (a decade) longer than those in 1970 experienced (that's less than 50 years or five days ago), thanks mainly to life-extending medical breakthroughs and a more evolved view on diet and exercise.

So things have changed. The 'future of work' (as discussed in chapter 10) will turn everything upside down over the next decade or so. Industries will be replaced or change shape and the way we work will alter dramatically. The digital revolution has ensured an exciting ride with plenty of thrills along the way. We also have that little problem of the baby boomers. They're the largest section of our community and they'll all be well into their weekends within the next decade. That's wonderful for them; however, they form the basis of the workforce, meaning they have been paying most of the tax over the past 50-odd years. The next generation might just need to come up with an alternative tax system to fund all these boomers.

So how does this affect the word 'retirement'? It blows that old framework out the window. Of course, we still have to save for our later years, but why is there pressure on people to save for a particular date—and then that's the end of their working week? We're sure some of you are saying to yourselves, 'I can't wait to retire'; 'I deserve it'. Well, yes, plan for that day, but don't be fooled into thinking you have to stop working just because that's what your parents did. Remember the psychiatrist's advice that stopping work can send you nuts—and then you die? A cautionary message, we think.

The three phases of rewirement

So, retirement has officially been retired. Rewirement is now the thing—and we should use it throughout our lives. We constantly have to re-wire ourselves: change tack, improve our money behaviour, measure how we're going and most importantly be ready to adapt. We have to find ways to receive an income for all the days of the week and into next week so we never have to worry about not having 'enough'. Savings is part of the tactic, of course, but it's not the only plan.

The rewirement strategy has three phases:

- *Monday to Friday is phase 1:* our highest exertion time
- *Saturday and Sunday are phase 2:* our lower exertion but highly relevant income phase
- *Next week is phase 3:* our time to enjoy some non-exertion income and ensure we stay healthy.

Income is important through all stages of our life, yet we tend to focus on this mythical retirement as the time when we stop earning income and start drawing down our savings. How can you have a sense of your required income in this mythical retirement period if you don't know what you spend now?

On what day do you think most people plan their retirement? Friday night! Late fifties. Why? Early in our week we don't see it as relevant. By the time we get to Wednesday we have a WTF moment. This means 'Wait Till Friday' to plan for the weekend. But by rewiring we don't have to wait. *So start now.*

If you're Wednesday now (thirties) you'll have a life expectancy of late nineties (nine days). Compare this to Wednesdays in 1970, who only had to worry about funding themselves for seven days. That's 20 years extra!

Have we got you worried? Well, good. We all have to wake up to the fact that we'll live longer than previous generations and that work has changed. Instead of putting our heads in the sand, let's work out a plan to be prepared for these three phases. Most of us don't pay any attention to our retirement savings. In Australia, superannuation is a magnet for apathy.

As we said, most people don't take an active interest in their weekend until Friday (fifties). That's very late in the week and Einstein's magical eighth wonder of the world — compound interest — is only magical if you give money time to weave its magic.

Let's look at how we can do that.

Phase 1

Improve your money behaviour and you'll have more funds as you reach the weekend.

Action:

Re-read this book.

Phase 2

The weekend should be planned for earlier in the week. However, if you're already closing in, it's not too late.

Action:

1. Improve your money behaviour by sleeping well, having a mindful money narrative and making baby-step changes.
2. Create side hustles that cause little exertion and more regular income.
3. Open your mind to learning new skills. Weekenders are highly sought after for their wisdom and work ethic. They get a bad rap for being too expensive to hire. Change that impression by cutting your costs and working the hours you want to work.
4. Understand the tax and superannuation system. Use it as a strategy to create a weekend that delivers income, and add to that some income-earning exertion. Defenders love the Australian superannuation system because it allows them to pay 15 per cent on their income rather than over 30 per cent. Yes, it's locked away, but that's a good thing because it protects Spenders from misusing it.
5. Prepare for phase 3 early. Next week (eighties+) has many trip wires and challenges, so set yourself up for next week on the weekend.

Phase 3

Of course, phase three is the time where you've placed a few non-exertion seeds that hopefully will flourish so you can enjoy a stress-free next week.

Don't retire and die, rewire and live

If you don't believe us, try to think of five people you know who have retired successfully. That is, they've stopped working altogether, and have enough savings to last them well into next week (eighties+).

Struggling to come up with five? Well, the reason for that is, it's not easy to retire successfully.

They say that there are only three benefits to being over 60 (Saturday):

- enjoying your grandkids
- having heaps of wisdom
- having time on your hands.

We say, that's not true because you're only just into the weekend and there's so much more life ahead of you!

Supplement your retirement savings

We looked at side hustles and personal exertion in chapter 10. This was more for those with limited time who wanted to prop up their income. For those winding down, the best side hustles capture the benefit of time and wisdom.

Here are some side hustles to consider for your weekend and beyond (60 plus):

- Participate in polls. Agencies are always looking for volunteers for their research. They pay for your time and you may get a free lunch.
- Become a tour guide. This combines walking, talking and your wisdom.

- Uber and Amazon (see chapter 10).
- Rent your car out. Rent your parking space.
- Rent your house out and live in a smaller rented place.
- House-sit. This usually involves looking after pets while busy families take off on holiday. It can be a great way to travel and meet people. Some of these gigs include free accommodation as well as payment.
- Expand into international house-sitting.
- Check out sites such as Airtasker to see if you have skills that can be hired out.
- Sell some of your possessions. It's liberating.
- Use your wisdom to tutor. If you worked for 40 years you will have skills even if it's teaching English or another language.
- Become a mystery shopper. You get paid to shop.
- Write letters to the editor. We know someone who writes letters on behalf of his dog. They're hilarious and he now has a blog that has led to advertisers. True story.
- Rent out all your tools and stuff. Your stuff might be just what someone else wants.
- Become an Airbnb concierge. Offer to let people in and out of Airbnb properties.
- Try becoming a tutor overseas. Perhaps teach English?

There are many side hustles for weekenders (sixties and seventies) and also for those in next week. Remember the old adage, 'If you don't use it, you'll lose it'.

Finally, seek some advice around how money works in retirement. Do some projections and get a feel for what you're heading towards. In Australia, most superannuation funds offer some form of advice regarding projecting your savings. There are also plenty of calculators out there that can assist you to get a sense of your own picture. The tax system, your personal circumstances, your spouse, your assets and your retirement savings all go into the mix.

A wonderful resource is moneysmart.gov.au.

The best advice we can give you is that no-one knows what they don't know. Oh, and the second-best piece of advice is don't WTF: don't Wait Til Friday!

Retired (and then rewired)

Wendy was 60 (Saturday) when she retired from a lifetime of nursing. She was tired and had dreamed of this day for many years. She loved caring but she didn't think her body could put up with the rotating shift work and pressure.

Wendy lives on her own and has a daughter living in Singapore with her family. Wendy was in a retirement fund that provided a reasonable return and she converted her plan to a self-funded pension. Wendy is a Defender and knows how to budget. She bought a small house in a rural area and was looking forward to life pottering around the house and joining some local community activities.

Within 12 months Wendy was bored and was plotting to murder some of her newfound community friends. Retirement was driving her mad. She was managing her money okay, but a sinking feeling was starting to blur her dreams. She started to realise she may just live for another 20 years (well into next week). Twenty years in a little community where everyone knows your name (like in the sitcom *Cheers*). She is well read and has a passion for photography.

Wendy's mental health was suffering. She started to feel anxious for the first time in her life. It hurt.

(continued)

Retired (and then rewired) *(cont'd)*

Wendy decided she needed to address her fear. She got some counselling and that led to her realising her fear was twofold: (1) She could outlive her money and (2) Is this all there is?

She decided to join an Intrepid photography holiday across eastern Europe. It was a big step for her, but she jumped in, hoping for the best.

What Wendy discovered on this trip was like-minded souls from across the world, of varying ages but all interested in photography and adventure. She met Matt, who was a Finnish nurse. He was also about to retire.

Wendy convinced Matt to avoid the rural community plan and together they decided to set up a travel page on social media for people like them who love photography. They were inundated with stories and developed a small, thriving blog providing travel and photography tips that attracts a bit of advertising revenue. A small income but with it came a sense of purpose.

The moral to Wendy's story is she solved both of her fears: purpose and making a bit of income, key ingredients for rewiring yourself towards the next chapter in your life. Wendy only needed a top-up to overcome her anxiety. She and Matt stayed friends (and never got under the spreadsheets) and Wendy is now a very happy person enjoying her rewirement.

Get into the habit of side hustling before you reach the weekend.

Retirement is so last century:

I don't wait for the weekend; I need to re-wire constantly.

The beginning

Welcome to your new relationship with money

We asked you to wait until you'd finished reading this book before making any changes. Well, now it's time to change your spenditude so you can create a more rewarding relationship with money to live the life you want.

Your next step entails considering each of the 11 New Realities introduced in this book, now that you have a complete picture of your spenditude and can self-describe your motivation for change. Because without change, there's a high chance nothing will happen.

When changing habits, it's crucial to ensure you document your motivation for changing, so for each New Reality, think about what motivated you to act on it.

We wish you great success in this life-changing exercise.

For more on spenditude visit spenditude.com

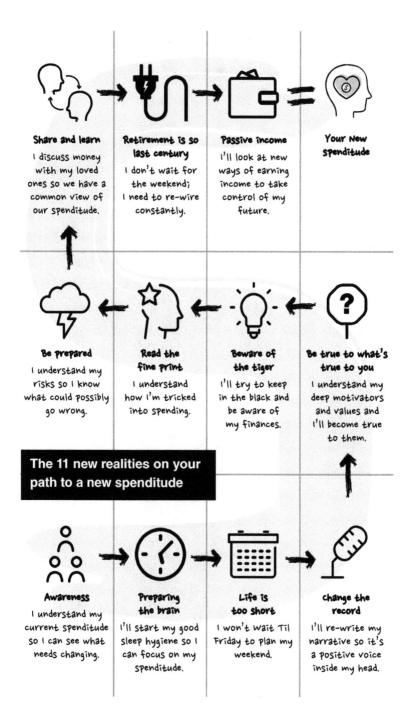

Share and learn
I discuss money with my loved ones so we have a common view of our spenditude.

Retirement is so last century
I don't wait for the weekend; I need to re-wire constantly.

Passive income
I'll look at new ways of earning income to take control of my future.

Your New Spenditude

Be prepared
I understand my risks so I know what could possibly go wrong.

Read the fine print
I understand how I'm tricked into spending.

Beware of the tiger
I'll try to keep in the black and be aware of my finances.

Be true to what's true to you
I understand my deep motivators and values and I'll become true to them.

The 11 new realities on your path to a new spenditude

Awareness
I understand my current spenditude so I can see what needs changing.

Preparing the brain
I'll start my good sleep hygiene so I can focus on my spenditude.

Life is too short
I won't wait til Friday to plan my weekend.

change the record
I'll re-write my narrative so it's a positive voice inside my head.

About the authors

PAUL GORDON is a reformed *Spender* with an enquiring mind. For most of this new century he has been zeroing in on the puzzling question: *why are some people better with money than others?* His first book *Uncommon sense from an Uncommon mind (2008)* started to answer this question and *Spenditude* continues to explore the real issue of habit change for a better life.

Paul has a passion for storytelling and consults to organisations around creating beautiful workplaces through financial wellbeing.

JANINE ROBERTSON has always been an organiser, list writer and planner. She has a passion for learning and her studies have focussed on financial planning and behavioural economics.

Janine is a working mum, with three young kids and a demanding career in which she has focussed on helping people bring more awareness to their financial position.

Janine would love to see more people aligning their money attitude to their real values and purpose.

Paul and Janine have a strong passion for helping people to improve their financial attitude and awareness. They are different ages and have different backgrounds but have a common belief that people fail to reach their financial potential due to behaviour, not income. They have worked together over the past 15 years to develop at-work financial wellbeing programs.

Connect with Paul and Janine at spenditude.com

Index

addiction 10, 17, 44–45, 121, 122–123
Airbnb 192–193
Airtasker 191
alcohol 37–38
AmazonFlex 192
anchoring 138–139
Andrew and Lucy's (spreadsheet) story 7–8, 26–27, 111–112, 171–172
Anna's story 21–23, 80–82, 101–102
anxiety 30, 63, 67, 108, 167, 214
artificial intelligence (AI) 196–197
Ashworth, Jairus 197–199
attitude to money 60–63; see also narrative, money; spenditude
—examples 63–65
awareness 107–133
—change and 123
—creating 108–109
—mindfulness 120–127
—plan and pivot 108–112, 132
—SANE Australia 123–124
—spend less than you earn 113–115
—understand compound interest 116–117
—wise investing 117–121

baby boomers 207
behavioural science 149–150
behaviour(s) 6, 44, 60, 123
—financial attitudes and 63–65
blue light, effects on sleep 39–40, 41, 42
blue light glasses 40, 41
BOGO marketing strategies 139–140
brain
—'baby brain' 166
—Defender 12, 45
—dopamine 69, 70, 109–110, 122–123, 137, 140

brain*(continued)*
—function 32, 44, 69–70, 71, 127
—sleep and 30–31, 33–34, 35, 42, 44, 45, 127, 217
—Slender 11, 14, 45
—Spender 10, 45
—structure 125
—training 30, 54, 62, 86, 109, 124, 125, 140, 185
budget 24, 64, 72, 73, 90, 113, 133, 148, 151, 177, 213
Buffett, Warren 117
buyers' remorse 70, 71
buying *see* spending

caffeine 38
categories of spenditude 5–8; *see also* Defender; Slender; Spender
celebrate small wins 111
change 111–112
—achieving 137, 147
—attitude and behaviour 87–89, 90–91
—behavioural science 149–150
—identifying the why 87–105
—money narrative 13–14, 59, 61–63, 66–69, 76, 81–82, 84–85, 88, 167, 217–219
—nudging 150

—small changes, making 109, 128, 150
cheerleaders 134
children
—focus 185–186
—identifying spenditude 183–185
—teaching spenditude to 183–187
childhood, effects of incidents in 176–177; *see also* children; parents, influence of
choices 140–142, 148–149
circadian rhythm 33, 34–35, 39
coffee costs 145–146
coffee drinking 156
cognitive
—decline 35
—dissonance 70–71
—function 45
cognitive behaviour therapy (CBT) 127
compound interest 116–117
cost points 145–146
credit *see also* debt; payment
—access to 9, 113
—cards 10, 22, 24, 25, 80, 116–117, 118, 119, 133, 148, 152
—use of 110, 132, 153

days of the week and money management 49–53, 69

death clock 143–144
debt
—attitudes to 113–114,
152
—good vs bad 118–120
—interest, paying
116–117
—keeping out of 111–112
—mortgage 119–120
—payment order 119
—payment strategies 119
—saving and 118
Defender category 11–12,
13, 113, 149, 152; *see
also* Andrew and Lucy's
(spreadsheet) story;
marriage; relationships
—brain 12
—cashbox 120–121
—debt 112, 119
—defined 5
—drivers 93, 100–101
—emotions 5
—goals 11
—habits 5, 21, 179–181
—lessons from 133–134
—lifetime 50–53
—Lisa's story 96–97
—marriage to a Defender
179–181
—narrative, money 74–75
—needs 99, 100–101
—parents 186–187
—Paul's dad's story 88–89
—rewirement 99, 100–101
—risk 164

—side-hustle 190
—spending 93, 94, 95,
113
—Tom's story 25–27
—values 100–101
—wills 157, 162–163
—work 201, 202
decision making 128, 142
—influences on 150–151
default options 141–143
Defender's cashbox
120–121
digital revolution 76, 108,
207
discount, asking for a 152
discretionary vs non-
discretionary spending
113–114
diversity 164
divorce 14, 15, 66, 171,
172, 174, 175; *see also*
children; marriage;
parents; relationships
drivers 91, 93–95
—Defender/Slender/
Spender 100–101

earning more 110
emergency fund 110, 118
emotions 2, 5, 37, 44, 109,
148–149, 152–153; *see
also* feelings and habits
—money and 95, 175
—money narrative 67,
176–177
—spending and 114–115

empathy gaps 142
estate planning *see* wills
exercise 37–38

feelings and habits 16–21;
  see also emotions
—Defender 5, 20–21,
  179–181
—Slender 5, 18–20
—Spender 5, 17–18
financial literacy 148–149
focus 24, 30, 31, 65, 66, 74,
  90, 99–101, 120, 123,
  143, 151, 185
—sleep and 43, 44, 45
food delivery 191
future self-continuity 142

gamification 132
gig economy 195–196
goals 11, 172–173
—rating 173–174
—setting 108, 109–110,
  128, 131
Good Return not-for-profit
  organisation 68–69
gratitude 134

habits *see also* change
—changing 87–105, 112,
  123
—Defender 5, 20–21,
  179–181
—Slender 5, 19–20
—Spender 5, 17–18
health insurance 140, 148

home sharing 192–193
Hooper, Justin 173, 175–176

Iceland, banks in 165
income, second *see* side
  hustle
Instagram following 193
instant gratification 23
insurance 20, 21, 121, 140,
  146, 148, 162–164, 200
investing, wise 117–121
iPhone mania 72

job board apps 191–192
journaling, financial 131

life insurance 162–163, 200
—in super fund 162–163
lifetime, as days of the week
  49–53
Lisa's story 96–97
loss 147, 152–153
—reframing 147–148

marketing tricks 137–140
—anchoring 138–139
—BOGO strategies
  139–140
—Goldilocks effect
  140–142
meditation 125; *see also*
  mindfulness
mindfulness 120–127
—awareness 123
—defined 123–124
—how it works 125–126

—money management
and 124–125
—self-awareness 126–127
marriage 26, 74–75, 171–
172; *see also* children;
parents; relationships
—Defender/Defender
179–181
—Defender/Slender 7–8,
26–27, 111–112, 171–172
—Spender/Defender 64,
171–172
—Spender/Slender 9, 24
—Spender/Spender 64–65
Maslow's hierarchy of needs
91–93, 94, 99
mindfulness *see also*
meditation
—children 185
—spending 124–125
money
—categorising 144–145,
152–153
—discussing 97
money-saving tips 131–135
motivators 93–99, 100–101
multitasking, avoiding 133,
153

naps 38–39; *see also* sleep
narrative, money 60–61,
176–177
—changing your 13–14,
59, 61–63, 66–69, 76,
81–82, 84–85, 88, 167,
217–219

—conflicting thoughts
69–71
—Defender 74–75
—financial outcomes 62–63
—old and new
soundtracks 61–63
—Slender 73–74
—Spender 71–72
—stocktake 84–85
—understanding your
66–69
needs 91–93
—Defender/Slender/
Spender 99, 100–101
—Maslow's hierarchy of
91–93, 94, 99
nudging 150

1 percenter rule 180
outsourcing 193, 195–196
overstocking, avoiding 134

pain 153–154
parents: *see also* children;
marriage; relationships
—Defender 186–187
—influence of 21–23,
23–24, 25–26,62–63,
64–65, 76–79, 96–97, 177
—teaching children
183–187
payment
—methods 146–147
—order of payment 119
—pain of 153–154
—time of 146

peak-end rule 70–71
planning pivot 108–112, 132
Pottenger, Chelsea 124–126
poverty cycle 68–69
price, appropriate 151–152,
153

reactions to financial issues
62–63
relationships and money
171–188; see also
children; marriage;
parents
—awareness 176
—children, teaching
183–187
—emotions 175
—fear 174
—divorce 171, 172, 174
—goals 173–174
—spenditude, discussing
171–172, 173–174,
177–178
—spenditude partnership
plan 172–177
—values 171–172,
173–174
—why 176–177
response to events 65,
66–69
retail therapy 10, 17, 121,
122, 126
retirement (rewirement)
205–219; see also
retirement savings;
rewirement

retirement savings 19, 134,
143, 162, 201, 202, 206,
208, 209, 211, 212–213
—supplementing 211–213
rewirement (retirement)
205–2019
—aged pension 206
—change in 207–208
—Defender in 213–214
—defined 205–206
—phases in 208–210
—side hustles in 211–212
—successful 211–213
—supplementing savings
211–213
—Wendy's story 213–214
ride sharing 190–191
risk
—Defender/Slender/
Spender 164
—identifying 157–159
—intestacy 159–160
—register 157–159
—women 164–167
Ryan, Mark 31, 32, 34–35,
126–127

savers, saving and savings
18, 19, 24, 25, 26, 75,
96–97, 110, 112, 121, 127
128, 131, 142–143, 144–
145, 150, 152, 180, 206,
208, 209, 211, 212–213
—debt and 118

—retirement 19, 134, 143, 162, 201, 206, 208, 209, 211, 212–213
—rounding bank balance 134
—tips for 131–135
security, financial 2, 4, 13, 16, 19, 20, 30, 65, 75, 80, 81, 82, 95, 96, 97
self, future 142–143
self, sense of 126–127
self-awareness 126
self-confidence 99
self-knowledge 99
self-reflection 126
self-talk 85
self-worth vs net worth 98–99
side hustle 189–204
—Defender/Slender/Spender 190
—defined 189
—gig economy 195–196, 197–198
—personal exertion 190–192
—very-little-exertion 192–195
—in rewirement 211–214
—sharing economy 190–191, 192–193
singles and money 181–183
sleep, influence of 29–48
—behaviour, effects on 32
—benefits of 36

—blue light effects 39–40, 41, 42
—change, achieving 29–30
—disruption and health 35–37
—improving 134
—importance of 31–32
—lack of 31, 37, 41
—money and 44–45
—naps 38–39
—phases of 33–35
—preparing for 32–33
—routine 38–39
—shift work 43–44
—teenagers 42–43
—tips for good 37–42
—tracking 45–46
—wellbeing 29, 31–32, 196
Slender category 10–11, 13, 14, 149; see also marriage
—brain 10
—Brett's story 76–79
—debt 112
—defined 5
—drivers 94, 100–101
—emotions 5, 18–20
—habits 18–19
—Jenny's story 23–25
—lifetime 50–53
—narrative, money 73–74
—needs 93, 99, 100–101
—risk 164
—side hustle 190
—spending 94, 95, 114
—values 100–101
—work 201, 202

social media side hustle
193–194
Spender category 8–10, 13,
14, 75148
—Anna's story 21–23,
80–82, 101–102
—brain 11
—debt 112, 119
—defined 5
—drivers 93, 100–101
—emotions 5, 9, 17–18
—habits 16–18
—lifetime 50–53
—Lisa's story 96–97
—narrative, money 70–72
—needs 93, 99, 100–101
—retirees 66
—risk 164
—side hustle 190
—spending 93, 94, 95, 114
—stories 15–16
—values 100–101
—windfalls 66
—work 201, 202
spending
—addiction to 121–123
—brain function 69–70
—cash, using 133, 153
—choice and 140–142
—Defender 93, 94, 95
—driver priorities 93–95
—drivers 93, 95–99
—emotions and 114–115
—fasting from 131
—foregoing 112
—intention in 115

—mentally discounting
146
—mindfulness and
124–125
—needs 91–93, 94
—non-discretionary
113–114, 121, 179
—passion 74, 113–114,
120, 121
—Slender 94, 95, 114
—Spender 93, 94, 95,
114
—tracking 90–1, 113–114
spenditude see also change;
Defender category;
Slender category;
Spender category;
—categories of 5–8
—changing 9, 13–14,
15–16
—days of the week and
49–53
—defined 1
—identifying your 3–5
—importance of 1–3
—nature of 1–28
spend less than you earn
113–115
staying on track 111
storytelling 75–76
stress 125, 150
subscriptions 134, 153
superannuation see also
retirement funds
—life insurance in
162–163

Thaler, Richard 150
Tight Tuesdays 131
timeline as a week 56–57
tomorrow account 128

Uber 190–191

value lens 11, 65, 74–75, 79,
    114–115, 144–145, 146
values 10, 89, 93, 95–99, 167
    —change and 93, 95–97
    —clarity around 98
    —Defender/Slender/
    Spender 100–101
    —determining your
    104–105
voice in your head 59–86;
    see also money narrative

wait till Friday (WTF) 51,
    143, 158, 209, 213
waste 20, 26, 61, 74, 75, 114,
    115, 147, 180, 181, 190
wealth creation 113,
    116–117
websites, comparison 148
why, understanding 87–105,
    176–177
    —outcome 99–101
willpower 150–151
wills 157–169
    —attitudes to 157
    —carer, providing for 161
    —importance of 159–160,
    164

—intestacy 159–160
—life insurance 162–163
women 207–208
    —entrapment, financial
    166–167
    —as investors 165–166
    —maternity leave 166
    —risks for 164–167
    —suggestions for. other
    194–195
work see also side-hustle
    —career ladder 198, 199
    —changing 205–206
    —Defender/Slender/
    Spender 201, 202
    —education, importance
    of 199
    —financial benefits
    200–201
    —future of 189–190,
    196–199, 202–203, 207
    —negotiating conditions
    of 200–202
    —personalised rewards
    201–202
    —reward programs 202
    —workforce change
    198–199, 206, 207–208